FOG CLEARANCE

Mapping the Boundary between
Coaching & Counselling

Paul Mooney PhD

IRISH INSTITUTE OF
TRAINING & DEVELOPMENT

Published by OAK TREE PRESS, Cork, Ireland

www.oaktreepress.com / www.SuccessStore.com

© 2015 Paul Mooney

A catalogue record of this book is available from the British Library.

ISBN 978 1 78119 210 8 (paperback)
ISBN 978 1 78119 211 5 (ePub)
ISBN 978 1 78119 212 2 (Kindle)
ISBN 978 1 78119 213 9 (PDF)

Cover design: Kieran O'Connor Design
Cover illustration: Carolyn Franks / 123rf.com

CONTENTS

ACKNOWLEDGEMENTS

Fog Clearance is the product of a collective effort over more than two years. A huge thanks (and a share of the blame) goes to the following:

- o **For posing the question:** Marina Bleahen, Veronica Canning, Brenda Dooley, Cathy Gilmore, Carol Jarrett, Suzanne Jeffery, Edna Jordan, Gary Joyce, Gerry Keenan, John Lennon, Pinar Rossiter and John Randles.

- o **For sharing their expertise:** Neville Bourke, Sean Brophy, Linda Brunton, Cathy Buffini, Mary Brennan, Declan Byrne, Avril Dowling, June Duffy, Kieran Duignan, Deirdre Giblin, Tom Jordan, John McGlynn, Michael Owen, Geoff Pelham, Jenny Stacey, Michael Stirling and Yvonne McWey.

- o **For encouragement and critique:** Maeve Donovan, Niall Hogan, Frank Kelly and Nial O'Reilly.

- o **For spotting mistakes:** (typos, grammatical errors and numerous other bits and bobs): Brian O'Kane and the eagle-eyed Oak Tree Press team.

- o **For sponsoring the book:** Sinead Heneghan and the Irish Institute of Training & Development.

- o **For putting up with the writing process (again):** Linda, Amie, Cillian and Nicole (my in-house supervisors).

Paul Mooney
Dublin, September 2015

FOREWORD

On behalf of the Irish Institute of Training and Development (IITD), I would like to extend a big congratulation to Paul on the publication of **Fog Clearance**.

You don't have to be a consultant or a Learning and Development professional to look forward to the ping of Paul's blogs on a Monday morning. We eagerly await our weekly input of 'Confessions of a Consultant' for his practical and relevant insights told in a humorous way.

Paul's ability to contextualise the theory into practical techniques and approaches is now delivered to us in **Fog Clearance**. Coaching has long joined the suite of high-impact learning and development interventions and forms an integral part of individual, team and organisational development. Coaching as a skill and a practice is not confined to qualified professionals but now is a core leadership competency; this book therefore is a 'must read' for anyone with people responsibilities or who has an interest in personal development and the development of others regardless of the relationship.

The role of the coaching professional is constantly evolving and client organisations and coachees have different – and higher – expectations of what coaching interventions will provide for them. There has been an accelerated pace of change – both in terms of subject matter expertise and pedagogical application – in this area, resulting in a heightened need to engage in an ongoing reflective process on how to evolve our understanding of coaching and how it differs from other interventions.

This is a unique book because it is aimed not just at coaches, but also at those responsible for sponsoring coaching interventions for a variety of other stakeholders. This book challenges us to self-assess our skill-sets as an effective coach and to explore ways in which we can better support coaching activity and achieve heightened outputs.

IITD is committed to providing thought leadership approaches and innovative solutions for learning and development professionals. As the body representing members at the forefront of human resource training and development in Ireland, we highly recommend that you not only put this book on your reading list but that you use it as a best practice guide regardless of the coaching role that you are engaging in.

Congratulations, Paul, and thank you for challenging us, informing us and inspiring us with **Fog Clearance**.

Nicola O'Neill
President, IITD

INTRODUCTION

EXPLORING THE CORE QUESTION

In recent years, there has been a virtual explosion in executive coaching.[1] Some observers rank this area as the fastest-growing 'product' across the entire people management arena, estimated by the *Economist* magazine as a global market worth somewhere north of $1 billion (June 21, 2014). A comprehensive UK survey (600+ organisations), found that 90% were using coaching delivered by internal staff while 60% contracted with external providers (CIPD, 2009). Yet, despite the growing popularity, the process is difficult to define; there's no simple answer to the question *'What is Coaching?'*. The central actors (buyers, clients and coaches) often have divergent views on coaching's core purpose. Adding to the confusion, the term *life coaching* is used without any agreement in the literature around how this is defined or differentiated from *coaching* or *executive coaching*.

Beyond *labels*, a more fundamental question is the difficulty of delineating the boundary line between coaching and counselling, the question that forms the central focus in this research. We begin our exploration by sketching the perspectives of the key actors.

Strand A: Buyer Confusion

Within organisations, buyers (often HR professionals) express the following concerns:

---

[1] The term *coachee* is used throughout to denote people who attend coaching as distinct from *clients* (people who attend counselling). The terms *counsellor* and *therapist* are used to identify people who have completed at least graduate-level training in psychology or psychotherapy. To assist readability, *he* and *she* are both used interchangeably rather than the clunky s/he.

o Are they spending resources wisely (does coaching deliver tangible business results?). While Linley *et al* (2006) suggests that efficacy (does coaching work?) is the most important question, as a practicing executive coach for over 20 years, I've never been asked to prove this. Similar to executive development generally, there is a belief that it can work, given the right coach / coachee chemistry.

o Will the process be developmental for the coachee, neutral at worst, certainly not harmful in any way?

o Should topics be business-related or is it legitimate to work on personal issues when the company is footing the bill? During a presentation made on the topic of coaching *versus* counselling to a group of HR practitioners (CIPD Christchurch, Dublin, October 2014), one of the audience members strongly made the point that personal topics – for example, relationships outside of work – were not legitimate in employer-funded coaching. It highlights a debate within the HR community around what should / shouldn't be on the coaching agenda.

Perhaps it's not surprising that buyers are confused about a process they cannot see (coaching meetings are conducted in private) and where, in most cases, there is no outcome (coaching plans or progress reports). Assuming that the process works, they should see changes in behaviour, but these are often subtle and difficult to detect. It follows that for many buyers, the purchase of coaching is akin to a religious experience; they have to believe in it (because it's almost impossible to prove it works).

Political Correctness

Buyers sometimes take a hands-off stance for another reason. Many are at pains to stress that they don't want to see outcomes in order to protect the confidentiality of the process. In this, they confuse means with ends. Of course, there is a necessary element of confidentiality in the face-to-face discussions (means). Trust is a fundamental requirement, allowing people to explore personal issues in relative safety, a boundary that needs to be respected for coaching to work. However, where the employer is footing the bill, arguably there is an entitlement to see the outcomes (ends) and determine whether the investment represents good value for money. She who pays the piper should at least hear the tune (at the top end, an executive coaching investment can cost €30,000 / €40,000).[2] There are very few areas where a high-cost purchasing decision is made on such frugal up-front information when the outcome is so difficult to determine.

Complex Decision

A final point around complexity needs to be added into the mix. The various psychology schools and tributary approaches in both coaching and counselling are difficult to disentangle. It's like figuring out the best mobile phone contract; there probably are differences, but it's extremely difficult for a non-expert to decipher these. Similarly, buyers are often confused about the range of coaching and counselling options that exist. Taken together, these issues create significant buyer confusion.

Strand B: Coach Confusion

Buyers don't have a monopoly on confusion; some coaches are unsure about how the process works. The multifaceted nature of coaching precludes easy classification (Ives, 2008: 104). A *Harvard Business Review* Research Report asserted:

> The coaching field is filled with contradictions. Coaches
> themselves disagree over why they're hired, what they do, and
> how to measure success (Coutu & Kauffman, 2009: 26).

Within the profession, definition questions continually emerge: Is the goal short-term problem-solving (Are coaches essentially the plumbers of executive development? Find the leak; fix it; get out)? Alternatively, is the central purpose of coaching to create space for reflective learning, which implies a longer-term impact (West & Milan, 2001)? In terms of style, should coaches tell or facilitate? And, when it comes to background, are the best coaches drawn from the ranks of business or psychology?

---

[2]   This is the cost of a coaching assignment with very senior executives in Ireland.
     In the UK / USA, coaching assignments can cost much more than this.

My personal interest in understanding the boundary between coaching and counselling was sparked during the completion of postgraduate studies in Business and Executive Coaching in University College Dublin. During the programme, some participants responded to exercises we were asked to perform along the lines of "I came to learn about Coaching. We seem to have strayed into Therapy". My initial reaction was judgmental: "What are you afraid of?". Yet, while there was certainly defensiveness, there was also genuine confusion, within a seasoned group with many years of coaching experience.

Strand C: Counsellor Confusion

In the UK, there have been some recent moves to put counselling services on a statutory footing for the purpose of regulation. Having a clear and comprehensive definition of counselling seems like a useful precursor. Yet, as one eminent counsellor notes:

> When challenged to provide a crisp, comprehensive and boundary-setting definition of counselling, we often falter (Sheppard, 2004: 6).

Certainly, clients don't always present with issues that fit into neat categories. Some counsellors and psychotherapists express a disdain for coaching, seeing this as 'therapy without the qualifications'. The belief is that anxieties and behavioural problems cannot be resolved without a deep understanding of the principles of human development. In this, they place significantly more weight on the importance of psychology rather than business training (whereas many coaches are drawn from a business background). In addition to the concern about coaching effectiveness, there is a belief that coaches themselves need support and supervision to avoid burnout, mirroring the support structures that exist in the counselling arena.

Who Delivers?

Adding to the confusion, coaching can be delivered by a range of players. Line managers or more senior executives in the same organisation (mentors) can coach. There's also coaching for teams and an Organisation Development movement towards the creation of coaching cultures where the central tenets (non-directive style, high-quality relationships) become embedded into day-to-day management practices (Jarvis *et al*, 2006: 10). The central rationale here is a movement from command and control to a more participative style of management (Anderson *et al*, 2009).

To make an apples *versus* apples comparison, this research focuses on coaches who operate independently, contrasting their work with counsellors / therapists who also operate independently.

MAPPING THE TERRITORY

In developing a deeper understanding of the topic, we address a number of questions:

- o Is executive coaching different from counselling?
- o What underpinning assumptions drive each approach? Do coaches have a concern around inadvertently straying into *therapy,* opening a Pandora's box that could have detrimental consequences for coachees?
- o Are the people who present for coaching *different* from those who seek counselling?
- o Are the *issues* that a coachee or client explores *similar or different?*
- o Is there a listing of issues that coaches *don't* address?
- o Are different processes deployed – for example, art therapy to surface deep-seated issues?
- o If coaches step across the *therapy boundary*, are they equipped with the depth of skill required to perform effectively in a very different arena?
- o Are different *timeframes (past/present/future)* in play? *"I often say therapy is about recovering and uncovering, while coaching is about discovering"* (Williams, 2003: 26).
- o If the *territory* for coaches is expanding (morphing into counselling), should training practices be elongated?

The answers to these questions allow us to establish clarity around each *field*.

Crossover Techniques

Within the coaching arena, there are different philosophies at play, ranging from a consulting *tell* model to completely non-directive approaches more often associated with therapy:

> While coaching has been immeasurably enriched by the injection of new ideas and techniques, it has led to increased confusion about the precise nature of coaching and what it is designed to achieve (Ives, 2008: 100).

In this argument, Ives drew heavily on the earlier work of Stober & Grant (2006).

To illustrate the complexity, one textbook lists 100+ coaching approaches for practitioners (McMahon & Archer, 2010). Interestingly, many of the suggested techniques *migrated* from counselling. For example, in *Power Music*, McGeever suggests that coachees suffering from depression should identify music they consider upbeat (2010: 28-30). Storing this in an easily accessible format – for example, on a smartphone – allows people to tap into an instant source of positivity, a process that's often deployed in counselling (Therapist U).

Central Point

Many techniques are seen to work equally well in coaching or counselling. And the migration of techniques and approaches is not one-way. Counselling has also been influenced by coaching, particularly *high-impact* practices designed to secure gains in shorter periods of time (Therapist W).

Embryonic Profession

A profession is defined as an area marked by a shared body of knowledge, with commonly-accepted standards of training and ways to test competency. It allows collegiate testing of theories, techniques and claims of efficacy *via* research (Cavanagh, 2005). While there's little doubt about the growing popularity of coaching, based on these criteria it's not yet a *profession*. Because of its longer (100+ years) history, counselling is well established and we might expect *a priori* to find more standardisation in concepts and practices. Following this logic, the relative *newness* of coaching might explain a more fluid *modus operandi*.

In reality, the assumption that each *profession* operates 'standardised procedures' is overstated. There is a wide variety of approaches in counselling, represented by a range of different 'schools'. Efficacy arguments *within* the profession, coupled with human ingenuity and creativity, has led to a range of approaches rather than a set of standard operating practices. Yet, despite the diversity of practice, within the literature there is agreement on one centrally important point: coaching is becoming more *therapeutic* in orientation (Judge & Cowell, 1997). A curriculum review of the main professional coaching training programmes available in Ireland (delivered by University College Dublin, the Irish Management Institute and June Duffy, an independent psychotherapist) highlights this. The promotional literature from these sources demonstrates a strong focus on the *psychology of coaching*, with very little emphasis on what might be termed the *other* elements (contracting, goal-setting, managing organisation politics, career-mapping, billing and so on).

Changing Economics

One suggestion put forward to explain the *incursion* of counselling techniques is that executive coaching is financially attractive. Hourly rates for coaching can be a multiple of up to seven times the rate paid to therapists (based on a counselling rate of €50 per hour *versus* an executive coaching rate of up to €350). But it's not a straightforward comparison. Counselling relationships typically last longer and the 'lifetime earnings' from an individual client may approach that of a coachee who has undergone a shorter *treatment regime*. Nevertheless, the general point holds that executive coaching is more financially-rewarding than counselling. With a ceiling on the absolute number of clients that can be seen each week, some therapists have begun to migrate into executive coaching to supplement their income. This 'economic transfer' has had the unintended consequence of *muddying the waters* along the boundary line between the two approaches (Coach O).

WORKING HYPOTHESIS

Coaching began as a *goal-oriented* approach, helping executives improve their current and/or future performance. The role of the coach was to support the development of specific goals and action plans. Historically, the distinctions between coaching and counselling were clearer (in the way that, say, dentistry and medicine are *separate* yet both fall under the broad umbrella of human health). More recently, the practice of executive coaching has shifted and taken on a more *therapeutic* orientation. As a result, coaching and counselling practices have become increasingly difficult to disentangle. This *blurring* between coaching and counselling creates considerable confusion, particularly with 'boundary-spanning clients' where the presenting issues do not fall into a neat, distinct category.

Central Tasks

To make this argument clearer, the research addresses three central tasks:

- o **Fog Clearance:** Provide a clear, practical definition of *What is coaching?* and *What is counselling?*, making each discipline understandable on a 'stand-alone' basis.

- o **Practice Overlap:** Clearly identify the *boundaries* between coaching and counselling, along with the challenges posed for professionals trying to navigate this space. While there are numerous studies of coaching and of counselling, there is a dearth of literature that explores the *links* between both professions.

- o **Going Forward:** Given these changes, outline the implications for the professional training of coaches in Ireland.

SETTING THE SCENE

THE EXPLOSIVE GROWTH OF COACHING

Several reasons underpin the phenomenal growth of coaching over recent years:

- o The development of a management cadre.
- o A focus on targeting discretionary effort.
- o A search for a way to implement skills learnt.
- o The changing business environment.
- o The perceived financial impact of coaching.
- o Social acceptance.
- o Executive appetite.

Management Cadre

In the UK, the virtual *explosion* of executive coaching has been detailed in several studies conducted by the Chartered Institute of Personnel and Development (www.cipd.co.uk). A centrally-important point is the growing professionalism of the *managerial cadre* and the corresponding growth in specialist teaching organisations (for example, the widening provision of undergraduate and post-graduate management programmes across the Irish university sector). Arguably, executive coaching is simply the *latest* method to support executive education.

While each organisation chooses its own selection criteria (some focus on newly-appointed executives; others require up to two years' service before an executive becomes eligible for coaching), the primary reason for engaging an executive coach is to invest in high-potential, future leaders. A minority of organisations use coaching as a *remedial intervention* for executives who are *struggling* (Purchaser C). Kiel *et al* (1996) estimated that 25% of executives who seek coaching are moving up within an organisation, 50% are increasing their leadership responsibilities and the remaining 25% are experiencing difficulties. One respondent suggested that some organisations use coaching to avoid managerial responsibility: *"Sometimes, you just need to have a hard conversation. You can't outsource that"* (Purchaser D) but this was a minority view.

Discretionary Effort

As the central rationale for offering coaching is to improve performance, the focus is on increasing motivation and releasing higher levels of discretionary effort (Jarvis *et al*, 2006: 18). Discretionary effort can be defined as:

> Making the sort of choices that often define a job ... the speed, care, innovation and style of job delivery. This behaviour is at the heart of the employment relationship (Purcell *et al*, 2003: 108).

Executive coaching contains the not-so-subtle message: "The organisation values you and encourages your development. In return, we expect you to perform at an even higher level". In the world of coaching, there's no free lunch!

Skills Implementation

In part, the growth in coaching can be explained by the *limitations* of traditional training methods. Managers exposed to new concepts during development programmes often lacked an *implementation* mechanism to put these into practice (Vicere & Fulmer, 1996). The historical *over-reliance* on classroom inputs has now given way to a much broader menu, including e-learning, secondments, external conferences and coaching. Gray (2006) suggests that coaching reflects an increasing *shift* towards informal, *self-directed* learning.

Behavioural change normally requires exposure to a new concept, coupled with subsequent practice and feedback. Coaching is a perfect vehicle for this 'concept-practice' model, a *safe arena* to discuss ideas and explore implementation successes and failures, what's been described as a "rehearsal for action" (Casey, 1996: 176). In short, it makes the bridge between the classroom and the boardroom.

Changing Environment

The business environment is evolving faster than at any other time in history:

> Increasing competitive pressures like globalisation, technology breakthroughs and changing workforce expectations ... have radically altered the arena in which organisations compete (Mooney, 2012: 18).

In response to this, executives have recognised the importance of lifelong learning. The acquisition of knowledge is an *enabler* in a period of rapid change. Seen in this light, coaching offers executives a way to keep skills honed and up-to-date with the additional benefit of *benchmarking*, as coaches become a conduit for insights into external best practice (Purchaser A).

Financial Impact

Alongside the primary *learning* task, coaching also serves a *governance* role, reducing the risk of underperformance. At higher reaches in an organisation (where executive coaching is targeted), the cost of poor performance can be acute. The US lawyer and former President of Harvard University, Derek Bok, said, "If you think education is expensive, try ignorance" (1986). While not often discussed, the *failure rate* for executives is surprisingly high, estimated by one source at 50% (Feldman & Lankau, 2005). Coaching modifies the negative financial risk of underperformance.

While several researchers have tried to quantify the ROI of coaching, this poses several methodological hurdles. In some cases, the evaluation of success is conducted by the companies providing the service:

> Although we are not questioning the veracity of the effectiveness ratings, it is in the self-interest of the consulting organization to find positive results (De Meuse *et al*, 2009: 119).

Caution is required in interpreting outcomes when research is conducted by stakeholders with a vested interest.

But there have also been a number of independent attempts to answer the question: *Does coaching work?*. One case reported by a Fortune 500 company suggested that coaching produced a ROI of 529%, boosted to 788% when the financial benefits of enhanced employee retention were included (Anderson, 2001). Another study claimed that ROI averaged nearly $100,000 or 5.7 times the organisation's investment in coaching (McGovern *et al*, 2001). As these numbers were derived subjectively (through retrospective questionnaires and interviews), it's difficult to draw firm financial conclusions. Arguably, data from such studies represents 'collective anecdotes' (MacKie, 2007: 311) with restricted usefulness in terms of scientifically demonstrating value.

A central difficulty in measuring ROI is that coaching is hugely dependant on how the *specific engagement* aligns with organisational requirements (Corporate Leadership Council, 2003). While some assignments have potential for great leverage (in financial or other *results)*, other coaching engagements focus on an individual's job satisfaction or aspects of a person's life outside of work altogether. Yet, while quantifying the financial impact of executive coaching remains a *challenge*, the growing number of organisations using this technique demonstrates its growing acceptance. While it may not be fully scientific, it's hugely popular.

Socially Acceptable

Social factors also have played a role here, particularly the shift towards coaching being seen as a *developmental* process. One respondent remarked:

> Twenty years ago I wouldn't tell anyone I had a coach because of the implication that I didn't know how to do my job. This has completely reversed. It's a badge of honour now (Purchaser B).

The opportunity to work alongside an executive coach has become analogous to the L'Oreal slogan: 'Because you're worth it'.

Consider the following vignette. Both my wife and I work from offices at the back of our house. When her counselling clients call, she generally asks me to "keep out of the way" to avoid any potential embarrassment. In contrast, when my coachees come to the office, they tend to be much more open and have no problem 'interacting' with anyone they meet.

While coaching is socially acceptable, therapy has some way to go in this regard:

> ... of all the illnesses that affect humans, mental illness is the least understood and the most feared and ridiculed. It is no surprise that many people with mental illness pretend that it does not exist or hide their symptoms from family and friends rather than confess to suffering (Nowers, 2006).

Executive Appetite

Arguably, a key driver of coaching has been the experience of people who have found the process useful. One respondent (Purchaser B) suggested that there is a novelty value – people want to try something *new*. However, my experience is that personal development approaches that don't add value soon disappear. The steady growth of coaching in the marketplace attests to its value, both to high-functioning individuals and those who need support during more difficult times.

In explaining the growth of coaching from the point of view of the *coachee*, four factors are particularly relevant:

- o Overcoming isolation.
- o Pinpoint support.
- o Offering challenge.
- o Reflective learning.

Overcoming Isolation

The Gallup Employee Engagement survey is widely used in Ireland. While the company does not release data on the exact number of client companies, estimates[3] suggest that this is the most popular survey tool in use. Based on a '12 Questions' platform, it allows

---

[3]   CIPD Dublin Office response, April 2015, to query by the author.

organisations to benchmark the level of staff engagement. One of the questions asked is *Do you have a best friend at work?* On first glance, the question seems somewhat *junior*, perhaps more appropriate to a survey aimed at second-level students. Yet the Gallup research highlights *isolation* as being a hugely important contributor to mental ill-health. Having a 'best friend' or confidant at work is fundamentally important to most of us. Executive coaches fulfil this exact role. Paris describes coaching as a sanctuary, a place where leaders "can remove their armour and lay down their defences" (2007: 121).

An article on emerging 'best leadership practices' (*Fortune*, November 2014) estimated that 90%+ of Fortune 500 CEOs (America's largest market-capitalised companies) currently work with an external coach / advisor. The coach – someone whom the executive respects and who has the ability to operate in a non-judgemental fashion – is increasingly seen as an important external member of the C-suite.[4]

Why? The CEO role is the *most isolated* in any organisation. The person occupying that chair typically cannot share their concerns. Because everyone else reports to them, discussing performance issues is *politicking*. Neither can they express uncertainty; *unsure* signals, while authentic (no-one is 100% confident all the time), are normally frowned upon at this level of an organisation. The CEO role is akin to that of an airline pilot. Neither pilots nor CEOs verbalise doubts; they are both *expected* to communicate *confidence* about the future. Coaching allows executives a *safe place to explore issues* in a supportive environment.

The core orientation of all coaches (and counsellors) is empathy; the role is to support clients, not *judge* them. To make this point explicit, I often say to coachees who have a (conscious or unconscious) fear of being judged, *"Relax. I'm working for you, not vice versa"*.

---

[4]   Chief Executive Officer, Chief Financial Office, Chief Operations Officer – collectively, the C-suite.

Pinpoint Support

Most senior managers have already attended college. Many have an MBA or other post-graduate awards in line with the quip "My clients have more degrees than a thermometer". It follows that executive coaching is seldom about *teaching* the '4 Ps of Marketing' or other rudimentary skills. Executives normally have a better understanding of their industry and organisation culture than the coach. The need is therefore for pinpoint support around specific issues that the executive is wrestling – for example, *How do I deal with a difficult Chairman?* or *What's the best way to make a presentation to a Dáil Committee?*.

In essence, this element of coaching represents a targeted, just-in-time development strategy:

> Completing training in a vacuum is ineffective. Unless
> information is used quickly, it evaporates (Purchaser B).

Offering Challenge

A less often reported aspect of the coaches' role is to *challenge* clients on their thinking and behaviour, memorably described as "speaking the unspeakable" (Hall *et al*, 1999: 40).

Several writers suggest that personal change comes at the edge of discomfort:

> ... the critical insight that allows shifts to happen come when
> those involved in reflecting on the challenges faced realise they
> are actually sustaining the very system they want to change
> (Reams, 2009: 173).

To successfully 'ego check' senior executives requires courage and some degree of skill as it has to be exercised side by side with empathy. While support is given, paradoxically, coaching can be a tough and sometimes disturbing process. Like going to the gym, coaching works best when executives (mentally) *feel the burn*. Some coaches feel the *correct* way to coach is to err on the positive side, based on the mistaken belief that being 'positive' at all times is the best way to increase a person's self-confidence. Yet no-one is right all of the time and coaches shouldn't collude with executives that they are an exception to this. In the real world that coachees inhabit, they have to learn to deal with the 'slings and arrows' of feedback, which is often negative.

Of course, a slightly darker force also can be at play here. Some coaches take a positive stance in order to ingratiate themselves, in an attempt to improve the likelihood of securing future business. These coaches should come with an attached health warning: *Danger: Collusion @ Work*.

Helping executives reach their full potential, by challenging their thinking or behaviour is not for the faint-hearted. Cavanagh (2006) captures this idea brilliantly when he suggests that therapy seeks to comfort the *afflicted* whereas coaching can seek to afflict the *comfortable*.

Reflective Learning

Executive roles, generally busy, can sometimes be *über*-stressful. Taking time out from the *pressure cooker* environment offers moments for guided reflection in organisations when there is often little time for this. This confidential learning process focuses on both interpersonal and intrapersonal issues (Witherspoon & White, 1996; O'Brien, 1997).

Several studies support the idea that executive coaching benefits both executives and their organisations (Olivero *et al*, 1997). Executives experience coaching as a positive endeavour, driving increased productivity and personal satisfaction (Hall *et al*, 1999; Gegner, 1997). Most of the professional research on coaching outcomes highlighted a positive response, with one commentator concluding that it provides a *psychological massage* for executives (Chapman, 2006: 188).

While the jury may still be out on whether coaching *works*, the question 'Do executives like coaching?' has already been decided. The answer is a resounding 'Yes'. Having demonstrated 'stickability' over the past 40 years, coaching cannot be dismissed as *'just another business fad'*.

Coaching Downsides

If coaching is *such a great idea,* it raises the question why more organisations don't deploy it? Several potential downsides along with some genuine misunderstanding around the coaching process help to explain why.

Securing Investment

Securing adequate training budgets is problematical in many organisations. Training & Development (T&D) staff often don't have a specific budget that they are empowered to spend. Normally, each programme is decided on merit against strong internal *competition* for the same resources. As the cost of executive coaching is substantial and it's not easy to quantify the outcome, it can be difficult to make the *business case.* While T&D professionals become familiar with *value for money* arguments, they're hampered by the fact that there is little empirical evidence to *prove* the value of coaching. Some of the evidence that exists is based on dubious methodology – for example, 'case studies' and self-reporting. While arguments can be made that executives who have been coached also become better at leading their own teams and some other *spin-offs,* these points are equally difficult to quantify. In marked contrast to the scientist-practitioner approach in psychology, a suspicion of rigorous evaluation is sometimes supported by those who profit from proprietary coaching models, not *grounded* by research (Grant, 2008: 24-25).

How Much Do Coaches Charge?

There was a range of responses under this heading. The *cheapest* coaching uncovered during this research was €125 per hour. The same coach charged up to €350 per hour and "everything in-between" based on a client's ability to pay.

The pricing question was a moving target with several of the coaches met. A number of coaches operated a two-hour minimum charge as an efficiency measure: "Driving into town and parking to conduct a one-hour session actually takes three hours" (Coach L).

In addition to their professional role, a surprising number of the coaches met also worked on *pro bono* projects (one insisted that people make a donation to the Society of St. Vincent de Paul on the basis that "free coaching is too easy to ignore").

Given the hourly cost and the elongated process, some T&D professionals feel that there is more 'bang for your buck' in traditional training programmes.

Remedial Coaching

Does the process *always* deliver? The evidence suggests that *remedial* coaching offers very mixed results. Some coachees are *sent* on the managerial equivalent of a trip to Lourdes – a *last throw of the dice*! While executives may have performed highly in the past, requirements can change and their impact can become sub-par.

Yet, when people *sent* for coaching are experiencing *difficulties* in an organisation, similar issues are often mirrored in the coaching itself. The *asks* at the heart of the process (achieving personal insight; establishing a deep relationship with the coach; being challenged on behaviour) are particularly difficult for *conscripts* (not *volunteers)* who erect barriers to protect themselves. All too often the reluctant coachee sees the coach as an extension of the management system. Indeed, the questioning and probing at the heart of coaching can be misinterpreted as *evidence of collusion* between the coach and the employer. Sometimes coaching is seen as Step 1 on the road to outplacement, with the employer building a 'watertight legal case'. Because trust is such a fundamentally important part of the mix, it's questionable whether progress can be made under these circumstances:

> Even if the coach is able to communicate an empathic, non-judgemental, and authentic stance ... if the client is unable to trust that the context is set up for his or her success, the likelihood of success is threatened (Stober & Grant, 2006: 359).

Where a person feels *forced* into the relationship, coaching may be doomed to failure (Latham *et al*, 2005). Clients who resist feedback, lack motivation to change or may have severe interpersonal problems or psychopathology also contribute to negative coaching outcomes (London, 2002).

The research evidence suggests that coaching is less successful when executives are defensive and unwilling to look inward, as distinct from situations of growth and personal advancement (Coutu & Kauffman, 2009). When a positive outcome can't be *guaranteed*, it's harder to *'make the sale'* for the substantial investment costs.

Unregulated Area

Executive coaching is unregulated; anyone can hang up their shingle and start practising. In one case reported, a finance director who'd been terminated the previous day *overnight* morphed into an executive coach (Smither, 2011: 141). To overstate, picture the following advertisement:

> Can't do your own job? Don't worry. Become an Executive
> Coach and tell other people how to do theirs. Start today. Zero
> training or investment required.

Without doubt, some of the scepticism around this area is a result of charlatans, the coaching equivalent of *cowboy builders*.

Consider the following. Some time ago, I sat next to a 'coach' conducting a live session in the lobby of the Maldron Hotel in Tallaght, Dublin. I'd arrived early for a meeting and, while waiting, listened to this very public coaching session. This coach instructed his female coachee to change her job, to become more positive and to log onto an Internet dating site which he seemed familiar with. Not bad for 21 minutes!

Overall, it's hard to damage someone by *listening* to them, but when it crosses the line and moves into giving *specific* advice in seven-minute time chunks, people should be cautious. That particular coaching session was about as useful as a fortune-telling visit to Gypsy Rose Lee (minus the excitement of the caravan and the crystal ball).

While no profession can fully *regulate for ethics* (presumably the accountants in Enron were qualified), some coaching derails rather than advances the careers of clients. While the research on this topic is light, the literature has recently defined and explored the concepts of marginal, dysfunctional and *toxic* coaching (Feldman, 1999; Ragins *et al*, 2000; Scandura, 1998). Some of the problems mentioned in this regard are the creation of dependency relationships, opting for quick fixes rather than taking time to properly diagnose needs (Noer, 2000) and breaches of confidentiality with the client company (Berglas, 2002). In similar vein, Kilburg (2000) identified several additional factors – for example, insufficient empathy, lack of expertise in the area of concern and poor techniques – that militate against a successful coaching outcome. In short, it doesn't always work. Coaching is not a 'magic bullet' solution to correct under-performance or to help people resolve life's dilemmas.

Nothing New

One final (sceptical) view about coaching is that it's the modern-day equivalent of 'The Emperor's New Clothes' (Tobias, 1996). The argument here is that coaching is simply *old wine in a new bottle*, a repackaging of techniques borrowed from other disciplines (counselling, psychology, consulting, etc.).

On one level, there's merit in this view; it is difficult to *separate* the various problem-solving and human development processes with a great degree of precision. But, to denigrate coaching on the basis that it's not something completely *new* is a weak argument. Tin and copper were around as single metals for a long time. When they were combined to produce bronze, a material with completely different chemical properties emerged. While many of the individual coaching techniques are not new *per se*, combining a number of these ideas has produced something new for executives with an appetite to take on the coaching journey. The *process* (an external person, dedicated to working with an executive on a confidential basis) is certainly new.

While some researchers view executive coaching with *suspicion* (Filipczak, 1998) or see this as a *passing fad* (Kilburg, 1996; Tobias, 1996), these are minority views. Executive coaching has become an accepted part of the managerial landscape. To explore why this is the case, we need to uncover what actually happens during the coaching journey. We begin at the beginning, cycling back to the fundamental definition: *What exactly is coaching?*.

DEFINITION: WHAT IS COACHING?

In simple terms, coaching can be defined as a *helping relationship* between an executive who has managerial responsibility and an external coach who has no formal role in the organisation (Kilburg, 2000). It's a *broad church*, embracing ideas from business consulting, psychology, sport and education (Stojnov & Pavlovic, 2010: 129). Even people steeped in the profession struggle to come up with a universally accepted definition that captures the array of approaches used (Stober & Grant, 2006). From a review of the literature, several themes emerge.

Master-Apprentice

According to Evered & Selman (1989), coaching emerged in the management literature in the 1950s as a master-apprentice relationship with the express goal of developing staff. Later, in the 1970s, several authors attempted to translate best-practice concepts from athletic and sports coaching into the management arena (McLean & Kuo, 2000; McNutt & Wright, 1995). Right up until the early 1990s, Druckman & Bjork portray coaching as *'guidance from an expert'* (1991: 61) while Hall *et al* (1999) define executive coaching as:

> A practical, goal-focused form of personal, one-on-one learning for busy executives that may be used to improve performance or executive behaviour, enhance a career or prevent derailment, and work through organisational issues or change initiatives. Essentially, coaches provide executives with feedback they would normally never get about personal performance, career or organisational issues.

As we will see later, feedback is an important part of the coaching mix; the metaphor of *'holding a mirror up to the coachee'* to accelerate learning is commonly used. This notion of *professional growth* is a thread that ties a number of coaching perspectives together – for example, Whitmore (2009: 97) suggests that the role of coaching is:

> Optimising people's potential and performance.

Evered & Selman (*op cit*) suggest that coaching is *"conveying a valued colleague from where he or she is to where they want to be"* while Burn memorably described coaching as: "A purposeful conversation that inspires you to create the life that you want" (2007: 33).

Types of Coaching

Cavanagh *et al* (2005) set out three *types* of executive coaching. The outcome in each case is that the *coachee* becomes more effective, consistent with the *growth* definitions offered above:

o **Skills coaching:** Coaching provides a *bespoke* solution, *pinpoint* training that targets specific skills / behaviours. Sometimes used as a 'getting ready' strategy for high-potential individuals, it is *tomorrow-* rather than *today*-focused.

o **Performance coaching:** Helps coachees set goals, overcome barriers and monitor their performance. Often used at a time of *transition* – for example, moving into a new job.

o **Developmental coaching:** Metaphor = voyage of self-discovery. Creation of a reflective space to address broader questions – it addresses *personal* along with *professional* issues.

Process View

If the core purpose is *growth*, how does coaching actually work? The answer is through a series of regular meetings between a business leader and a coach with the goal of producing positive changes in thinking or behaviour, in a limited timeframe (Corbett & Colemon, 2005). In terms of what actually happens at each *stage* of the process, the sequence is detailed below (*caveat:* the normal ebb and flow of a relationship is seldom linear; coaching is often *messier* than this):

- **Goal-setting:** At the start of the process; sometimes revisited mid-contract.

- **Obtaining feedback:** One-on-one; 360^0; psychometrics; data collection with line manager / HR.

- **Action planning:** Deciding how to move forward. Focus on *doing.*

- **Structured exploration:** Both parties discuss what's happening as the process unfolds.

- **Trouble-shooting:** "What happened when you tried to ...?".

- **Reflective learning:** Key lessons from the coaching process. Evaluation.

Coaching Themes

Another way to consider how executive coaching works is to review the topics addressed. Consider the following common coaching themes listed in the *UCD Post-Graduate Diploma in Business / Personal Coaching Handbook:*

- Learn a new skill / grow a capability.

- Solve a problem.

- Prepare for a future leadership role.

- Improve an aspect of personal performance.

- Make an important business decision.

- Improve a working relationship.

- Adapt your management style.

- Change some aspect of self.

- Address some unfinished business or 'baggage' affecting your work.

- Become more strategic.

- Develop your vision.

- Become a more effective leader.

o Develop your career.

o Achieve better work / life balance.

o Find greater meaning and purpose in your work.

o Find out what you really want from your life.

o Make a major life change.

o Improve your self-regulation.

o Develop your emotional intelligence.

o Make a behavioural change.

o Develop deeper self-belief and confidence (Pelham, 2014).

The enormous variety in the 21 items listed raises several questions:

o Is coaching a single process or are there a variety of approaches under this umbrella heading?

o Can a standardised 'one-size-fits-all' process address this *range* of topics?

o Finally, when the core topic is *learning*, how is coaching different from training?

To help dissect these issues, it's instructive to turn our attention away from *what* coaches focus on towards *how* they work - exploring the underpinning coaching philosophy.

Non-Directive Rules OK?

A central edict to coaches in most of the more recent textbooks is to *avoid giving instruction*. The emerging role for the coach is now understood to be *facilitative* – the coachee sets the agenda and resolves the issue. This is in stark contrast to the 'expert' role detailed earlier. In short, there has been a philosophical sea-change over the past 30 years (emerging metaphor = *'Give a man a fish and feed him for a day; teach a man to fish and feed him for a lifetime'*). Parsloe & Wray (2000, 47) argue:

> The more rapidly a coach can move from a hands-on to hands-off style, the faster improvement in performance will be achieved.

So, does this non-directive idea work well in practice? My personal experience is that coaching is not a *single way of working*. Differences in approach can add real value, including being *very directive*. To illustrate this centrally-important, but somewhat controversial point, two short case histories are sketched below.

Case Study A: Public Speaking

Tina Travis[5] wanted to address her fear around public speaking. She'd been promoted into an Investor Relations role that required extensive international travel. The job: to *sell* the company to a range of external investors whom she described as *"heavy hitters"*. With almost 10 years' experience in the industry, Tina was confident. She *knew the game*, had a sharp mind and a good sense of humour. Sometimes her boss would be present during the presentations, which added to the pressure to perform. During our first meeting she described the anxiety: "This stuff is really important. I don't want to make a balls of it".

Initial Response

In coaching, the first port of call is always to listen, both to demonstrate empathy and ensure that the *brief* is understood – what exactly is being requested? In addition to the outward *presenting issue,* was I missing anything? Might the concern around presentation skills mask a deeper issue – for example, a lack of self-confidence or fear of authority figures? Tina assured me that she wanted to work on this single topic, nothing else.

The Work

Over the next couple of weeks, I *taught* Tina how to speak in public. Many years ago, I learned a formula for public speaking and subsequently used this in a variety of in-company and public settings. We met six times, with Tina completing homework in-between meetings. At each session, she would *present* on a selected topic using a variety of media. My role was to critique the successive

---

5   Names and biographical details in all case examples have been changed to
     protect confidentiality.

presentations in an encouraging way. We had good fun, Tina became proficient and the coaching finished at that point.

This Doctor / Patient model was certainly *directive*. Yet, in terms of outcomes, Tina was happy that the *problem disappeared* and I was happy to support her. The case is reminiscent of the often-repeated quip from Warren Buffett on how the academic community regards his investment approach:

It may be all right in practice, but it will never work in theory.

So, should this *teaching model* be deployed by coaches all the time? Unfortunately, it's not that simple.

Case Study B: Life Purpose

Mike Mulcahy was in the process of *re-thinking* his life. A successful professional, he wanted to *connect* with his true path, essentially to figure out how the *next chapter* could be made fulfilling. Mike felt certain that the choices made thus far in his life had been less than optimal. This existential agenda covered a wide territory: career, finance, relationships, family and health. His reassessment followed a marriage break-up, which had significant emotional and practical fallout (childcare arrangements, sale of the family home and so on).

During the first session, I focused on understanding how Mike was *today* and contracted around topics we might usefully explore. As the sessions unfolded, we traced back over his earlier life. I wanted to help him process feelings about significant emotional events that had occurred.

Despite the fact that he'd initially presented with "My life is screwed-up", Mike eventually came to a view that there was lots of good news, running in parallel with the bad. Links with his parents and siblings were positive. He was well-regarded in his profession and had a high income.

Yet the marriage breakdown, coupled with a deteriorating relationship with his children (*teenage* issues were also in the mix), led Mike to over-focus on the immediate negatives. In psychology, the 'recency effect' explains how people *believe* that recent negative events have a disproportionate impact on happiness. In terms of *coaching style*, this was not a question of telling Mike what to think, of somehow *correcting him*. This *good parts and bad parts of my life* idea slowly unfolded.

Alongside this *archaeological dig,* I wanted Mike to feel *valued* in our relationship, free to express himself without fear of judgement. Creating this *safe space* allowed us to explore difficult and confusing issues. For example, Mike was conflicted around whether it's possible to both love and hate some aspects of your children *at the same time*. For my part, I wanted him to understand that many of us struggle to make sense of the dispirit parts of our lives; not every family is a mirror image of the Waltons!

With this foundation work completed (and checking that he felt ready), we began to address how the *next chapters* could be made more fulfilling. To focus on the *future*, I used a structured exercise to guide Mike in the construction of a life plan. Conscious of Van Deurzen's instruction that *"nobody else's purpose will do"* (2002: 43), we needed to find a method that had real meaning. As we worked through this phase, Mike really engaged in the construction of the plan. With a strong engineering-orientation, he enjoyed exercises that had a clear beginning-middle-end rather than ideas he deemed overly *philosophical*.

My role was to encourage him to complete the task. I didn't critique the decisions being made, some of which were quite radical. In just over one year, we met nine times.

Flexible Methodology

With Tina, my job was to *teach* her how to make effective presentations. With Mike, I was a trusted Sherpa. While this was an *expert* role (I designed the process and guided him along), it was *non-directive* in the sense that Mike decided how the next chapters in his life would play out. These were two very different examples of coaching.

As can be seen from the above (and will be demonstrated in later cases), coachees bring diverse *issues* that don't automatically fit into a narrow frame of *improving work performance*. In turn, coaches become deeply involved in the lives of coachees, with all the richness and complexity that implies. In order to deal with the variety of presenting issues, I believe that coaches need to offer a range of responses across the directive / non-directive divide.

And, this is precisely where the confusion arises. Because this idea – being able to swim in both the 'shallow' and 'deep' ends of the pool – raises a centrally important question: *When do coaches 'step over the line' and move into counselling?*

Is Coaching the Same as Counselling?

Just as wine packaged in a cardboard box is the same as wine sold in a bottle, coaching and counselling are sometimes seen to be different *labels* for the same *product*. Following this logic, if coaching is essentially *the same as* counselling, then similar principles should apply in both arenas. For example, in counselling there is a long tradition (and wide acceptance) around 'not telling' a client what to do.

The non-directive rationale is based on the following: Everyone has, within them, the ability to create meaning in their life and resolve their own problems. For example, clients presenting with *anxiety* or *coping issues* need to be empowered and become self-sufficient. *Telling* clients doesn't work and even has significant negative potential – for example, it can *re-create* a dysfunctional dynamic from the client's earlier life and actually worsen their situation, making them feel helpless, hopeless or both. Some clients, looking for support, will already have tried a number of solutions, everything from prayer groups to visiting astrologists (Therapist W). It's critically important not to present a quick fix, something that's externally imposed and potentially short-lived.

If this core *philosophy* (being *non-directive* is much more than a *technique*) has a solid rationale in counselling, shouldn't the same idea apply in coaching? The short answer is *yes and no*.

People who present for *coaching* can be on very different journeys as illustrated by the earlier cases. When the presenting issue is learning, coaches can usefully *instruct* – accelerate learning by sharing information or directly *training* coachees. In mathematics, the shortest distance between two points is a straight line; the same principle can apply in coaching. However, working with another coachee (or with the same coachee on a *different topic*), may require a much less directive approach – for example, the Mike Mulcahy case. Here, coaching is closely aligned to counselling and using a therapeutic (non-directive) approach makes perfect sense.

At this juncture we can make the following assertions:

o **Coaching ≠ Counselling:** While coaching and counselling have a degree of overlap, they are separate processes that are distinguishable (this will become clearer when we review counselling in more detail).

o **Coaching = Continuum of Support:** Coaching is an umbrella term that captures a range of methods. As the *presenting issues* can be very diverse, the coach needs to be able to respond in a *customised* fashion. Based on this research, this nuanced approach to coaching can usefully be grouped into two broad categories. In *Instructional Coaching*, the primary focus is on facilitating practical changes rather than psychological adjustments. In contrast, *Therapeutic Coaching* deals with deeper issues that go beyond 'New Year's Resolutions'. This sub-division of coaching fits well with the argument put forward by Ives who posits: "… the field of coaching would benefit by more overtly recognising that it incorporates quite diverse paradigms" (2008: 100). While the categorisation suggested is broadly in line with Summerfield's (2002) distinction between 'acquisitional' (acquiring a new skill) and 'transformational' (undergoing personal change) coaching, the 'instructional' and 'therapeutic' labels provide a clearer indication of what's actually taking place in the relationship.

Instructional Coaching

We saw earlier that coaching emerged as a *directive* (expert) process. The methods commonly deployed – short-term goal-setting, providing direct feedback and teaching – were *speedy* interventions designed to lead to quick resolutions.

An important point here is that instructional coaching is additive, essentially *bolting* a new skill onto an existing system. At a cognitive level, if I learn from *within* my current state, it doesn't change me as a *person*. Instructional coaching is a good fit with what has been labelled *horizontal learning*; in contrast, during *vertical learning*, the person stretches to learn something *new* (Kegan & Lahey, 2001).

Therapeutic Coaching

In recent years, the practice of coaching has become infused with ideas *imported* from counselling. Here we can detect a general movement towards what Bluckert has described as the *psychological dimension* (2006) and Gallwey has labelled the *inner game* of coaching (2010).

The arguments in favour of therapeutic coaching and the *deeper excavation* around what's happening for the coachee that this approach implies are as follows: At the heart of coaching there is an existential paradox; the *usual way* of doing things (thinking, feeling, behaving) is what got the coachee *here*. Yet, when executives take on new roles / challenges (for example, a finance specialist becoming CEO), the goalposts shift.[6] Success can move from a technical understanding of, say, finance to motivating and developing others. In some cases, the executive's *strengths* (for example, attention to detail) might even block success in a new environment. Seen in this light, coaching is not just about learning a new skill but can challenge a person's fundamental *way of being*. One source described this as follows:

> Coaching isn't for those who like to retreat to a darkened room
> and drape a wet flannel across their forehead (Keddy & Johnson,
> 2011: 12).

A key differentiation here is between *technical* and *adaptive* change. Technical changes are relatively easy to accomplish – for example, a lawyer boning up on a new piece of legislation, essentially learning *more of the same*. Adaptive changes are of a different order, *heavier lifting* requiring a shift in thinking, behaviour or both.

It follows that therapeutic coaching is much closer to counselling. Both *approaches* share a number of underpinning assumptions and use common methods. In one survey of coaching practice, 69.7% of practitioners described their approach as *facilitational versus* 17.4%

---

6   Geoff Pelham, UCD, in conversation with the author, November 2013.

choosing *instructional*. A central point is that these labels are not either / or. While coaches may have a predominant style, this does not stop the coach providing input and information at the appropriate juncture (Whybrow & Palmer, 2006). In short, the effective coach knows when to swim across the different levels in the pool as required.

The Elevation of Therapeutic Coaching

Arguably, the origins of coaching (instructional) have become somewhat *overshadowed* by the emergence of therapeutic coaching, which is much closer to counselling. Ives suggests a three-phase chronology as follows:

> ... coaching was directive, conceived as guidance, teaching or instruction. As coaching emerged as a distinct discipline, it was regarded as a form of facilitation ... and strictly non-directive. Increasingly, however, coaching has adopted therapeutic and personal development elements (2008: 103).

By focusing on the latter part of this *evolution*, some coaches have come to regard *directiveness* as incompatible with coaching. As coaching professionals edge closer to the therapeutic model, the benefits of instructional coaching have been *downplayed*. The notion of a coach as advice-giver has become controversial and *telling* is anathema to some practitioners (Grant & Stober, 2006: 363). One senior executive coach articulated this as follows:

> You can't change anyone else. You can only change yourself.
> Telling is not coaching. It's not even close (Coach N).

This criticism implies that there's one-best-way to coach. Earlier models are out-of-date, even *illegitimate*. Yet, the outcome of this field research demonstrates that coaching is more nuanced. There is no single mechanism to *"Hoover up unhappiness"* or to help people achieve their full potential (Therapist X). While traditional (instructional) coaching is sometimes dismissed as *swimming in the shallow end,* there's nothing inherently wrong with this. Indeed, swimming in the *deep end* sometimes leads to a condition called drowning!

Where coaches avoid being directive (*telling*), is this because it's the wrong approach for the coachee or a form of *political correctness* on their part? While coaches have much to learn from the world of counselling, my strong sense is that we shouldn't simply ape the methods developed and deployed in a different arena. These musings are critically important because the instruction 'not to do' something (*don't be directive*) can make coaches less certain. The ambiguity and confusion about this aspect of the role, coupled with the *elevation* of psychological training, has the potential to diminish coaches' self-confidence. It downplays and undervalues the impact of the coaches' prior business experience, which can be hugely valuable to coachees.

Based on this research, there is a continuing role for instructional coaching as part of a *menu* of offerings. The headlong rush into therapeutic coaching as a sort-of 'high end' practice, risks the loss of key benefits of instructional coaching – for example, clear focus and speed.

Determining the Dance

Coachees present with a wide variety of issues. To provide a *customised* response, coaches need an extensive toolkit (both instructional and therapeutic) and the ability to determine which *approach* to deploy. But the suggested 'dual approach' is not simple to operate. My experience is that people dislike ambiguity and normally prefer when the rules of engagement are *black* or *white*. However, the nature of coaching is uncertain, a '*dance along a grey line*', that stretches from consulting / tell (instructional coaching) across to completely non-directive (therapeutic coaching).[7]

The downside of being overly directive in every interaction is crystal clear. Most people are expert in their own world and don't need help to navigate this. Too much *sharing* of the coaches'

---

[7]   Some writers argue that the stance adopted by the therapist needs to *dovetail* with the client's personal change journey and suggest further sub-divisions – for example, nurturing parent, Socratic teacher, experienced coach and consultant (Prochaska & Norcross, 2001). While intellectually this point is consistent with the *no-one-best-way* argument, there may be an upper limit to the number of separate roles that a coach can play – the *suggested* steps in this *dance* may be too complex for most coaches to follow.

expertise can degenerate into a *tell* model in which the coach inserts himself into the role of *hero*. Yet, when the goal is to accelerate learning, at times it can be wholly appropriate (and ethical) to share the coach's expertise.

It follows that this *dance* needs to be determined on a case-by-case basis. A newly-minted executive facing his first boardroom presentation may need more support than a more seasoned player seeking promotion.

In order for the coach to be authentic (the *baseline* condition for solid work to be achieved), there's a need to avoid putting the professional in a *methodological strait-jacket* (Rogers, 1967: 185). This is even more potent when that strait-jacket is second-hand as it previously belonged to another profession (counselling):

> The skilful and experienced coach knows when to move across
> the ask-tell dimension and knows when to promote self-
> discovery and when to give expert-based authoritative or
> specialized information (Grant, 2008: 34).

In short, coaches need to know when to *tell* and when to *listen*. They need to decide when to put forward *process* suggestions, when to be engaged in *content* discussions and when to do absolutely nothing (other than being 100% present and empathic). They judge when it's appropriate to intervene *now* and when to revisit a point later, *"striking when the iron is cold"* (Yalom, 2005: 241).

Some people who attend for coaching are on a straightforward mission – for example, asking "What's a logical career step for me?". Others, searching for solutions to BIG life questions, embark on a more ambiguous journey. Working out a bespoke method (*dance*) to suit each coachee, makes the practice of coaching both intriguing and difficult.

The central argument here is that coaching is not formulaic, where each ingredient is weighted like a baking recipe. Without doubt, less experienced coaches require a *method*. The *caveat* is that the 'method' should not become a thinking substitute, a sequence blindly followed. This idea is neatly captured in the following:

When you're learning to ride a bike, you cling onto the handlebars. But, when you're great at cycling, you can let the handlebars go (Coach G).

In similar vein, Buber argues:

Without methods one is a dilettante. I am for methods, but just in order to use them. Not to believe in them (1967: 154).

One respondent spoke about the lemming-like danger of blindly following 'method':

We did a training course and the instructor drew three circles on a flipchart. A big outer circle with two smaller ones inside this. The idea was that the person was to write in the names of the people who were closest to them - they themselves were represented by a dot in the middle of the circles. So I tried it with one of the recovering addicts. He couldn't come up with anyone. After about 20 minutes he put the name of his dead granny on the flipchart. It was one of the saddest moments I've ever experienced (Therapist Q).

Default Style

There is a counter-argument to the above: while outwardly plausible, customising a style / process to suit the coachee is *impractical*. Coaches tend to adopt a default style and apply this to *everyone*. In recognition of what we might usefully label the *standardisation principle,* coaches should err on the non-directive side, steering well away from *telling*. There's a certain 'horse sense' to this argument. It's certainly easier to have a *standard* way of operating, something that runs on *automatic pilot*. If a coach was to err, arguably leaning towards *listening* has less damage potential than leaning towards *telling*.

However, the fact that it's *easier* to operate in a particular way doesn't mean that it's *better*. It's easier to learn how to ride a bicycle than to drive a car, but not necessarily superior. An analogy here is playing jazz, which lacks the precision of classical music where the exact sequence of notes and tempo are prescribed. In similar vein, coaching is a sort of *interpersonal jamming*. It sits between the *black (instructing the coachee what to do)* and *white (never telling the coachee what to do)*. Yet, even jazz players have to adhere to certain *rules* – for example, playing in the correct key. So too in coaching.

No-one who has worked in this space would suggest top-down, autocratic coaching as an optimum approach, except in very limited circumstances. However, the polar opposite idea – that a non-directive approach should be applied to all clients regardless of the *presenting issues* – is, in my experience, a massive over-correction. Grant & Stober take up this point with the succinct argument that a skilled coach knows when it is appropriate to act with authoritative expertise and when to act as a facilitator (2006: 363).

What emerges from this research is a view of coaching as a *range* of responses. The effective coach chooses an ideal response from a *toolkit* of potential methods. To make this concept work, coaches need to be able to tolerate a high degree of ambiguity. The practice of coaching is nuanced, a drive along an ambiguous line that, at times, can be extremely difficult to navigate.

Case Study C: Organisation Restructuring

Karen Kennedy, promoted internally, was tasked with running a large medical department. My coaching brief was to help her settle into the new role. The contract was strictly time-bound, limited to three meetings. Given the restricted timeframe, I decided to work with *whatever happens in the room,* sometimes labelled *free rein* coaching (Keddy & Johnson, 2011: 45).

During our first meeting, I helped Karen prepare for a meeting with her new boss. Our second meeting focused on an organisation restructuring project. In the first two meetings, Karen seemed to be playing a *new girl on the block* role – she didn't want to suggest anything *controversial*. Quite open about the performance of her own department (both good and bad news), she was much less comfortable when we looked *over the wall* at how other departments were functioning. An early indication was that Karen needed to work on her self-confidence. During our third and final meeting, we explored that topic in some depth. Later, she decided to progress this and completed a post-graduate qualification in management.

This assignment straddled both the instructional and the therapeutic models. While it involved some *technical expert*ise (organisation restructuring), the core focus was helping Karen to come to terms with the centrally-important elements in her role. Proactively managing the relationship with her new boss and becoming a strong member of the senior team (rather than being apologetic about her place at the executive table) were the central issues.

The short nature of the contract and the diversity of the issues tabled highlight the difficulty of following a *pure* coaching model in the commercial world. While hardly scientific, *you do the best you can in the time you have.*

Working Optimally

As part of this research, I asked both coaches and counsellors to describe a time when they were working optimally, at their very best. What were they doing? The answers were remarkably similar across the divide and related to 'being in the moment':

> I lose anxiety about being a coach that has to perform and deliver.

> I hear what the client is not saying. I'm in tune with my own feelings and pick up what they might be feeling.

> Everything just feels right. I feel mutual trust and time seems to move very quickly.

This suggests that the process becomes instinctive. The coach / counsellor is not constantly asking "Am I following the correct model?". Yet, while this 'automatic pilot' point is accepted, very different philosophical ideals underpin the instructional and the therapeutic coaching approaches. Hopefully, this has become clearer in the analysis presented above.

At this point we can usefully turn the spotlight onto counselling and consider how it works. We begin at the beginning, attempting to define this by posing the outwardly simple question *What is counselling?*.

DEFINITION: WHAT IS COUNSELLING?

In 1986, the British Association for Counselling (BAC) published the following definition:

Counselling is the skilled and principled use of relationships to facilitate self-knowledge, emotional acceptance and growth and the optimal development of personal resources. The overall aim is to provide an opportunity to work towards living more satisfyingly and resourcefully. Counselling relationships will vary according to need but may be concerned with developmental issues, addressing and resolving specific problems, making decisions, coping with crisis, developing personal insights and knowledge, working through feelings of inner conflict or improving relationships with others. The counsellor's role is to facilitate the clients work in ways that respect the client's values, personal resources and capacity for self-determination.

In their *Dictionary of Counselling* (1993), Feltham & Dryden offer:

Counselling is a principled relationship characterised by the application of one or more psychological theories and a recognised set of communications skills, modified by experience, intuition and other interpersonal factors, to clients' intimate concerns, problems or aspirations. Its predominant ethos is one of facilitation rather than of advice-giving or coercion. It may be of very brief or long duration, take place in an organisational or private practice setting and may or may not overlap with practical, medical and other matters of personal welfare. It is both a distinctive activity undertaken by people agreeing to

occupy the roles of counsellor and client and it is an emergent
profession ... it is a service sought by people in distress or in
some degree of confusion who wish to discuss and resolve these
in a relationship which is more disciplined and confidential than
friendship, and perhaps less stigmatising than helping
relationships offered in traditional medical or psychiatric
settings.

Later, in 1997, the Governing Council of the American Counseling
Association suggested the following:

Counselling is the application of mental health, psychological or
human development principles, through cognitive, affective,
behavioural or systemic interventions, strategies that address
wellness, personal growth, or career development, as well as
pathology.

Given these all-encompassing definitions, it's difficult to say what, if
anything, lies outside the scope of counselling. Similar to the
argument that coaching and counselling overlap, here we see
definitions of counselling that overlap with psychiatry (other than
prescribing medication, there is arguably an enormous crossover
between counselling and psychiatry). Indeed, Feldman & Lankau use
the term 'diagnosable pathology' to describe the issues brought for
resolution to therapists (2005: 829).

If we strip away the verbiage, counselling essentially can be
defined in shorthand as 'helping people with emotional or
behavioural problems to deal with these and lead a more fulfilled
life'. Sigmund Freud was realistic in describing what could actually
be achieved, noting that the goal of psychoanalysis was to *"turn
neurotic misery into ordinary human unhappiness"* (Hardingham,
1998: 96).

A centrally-important point is that therapy is not homogenous.
There are wide variations in practice among different schools and no
'one-best-way' to help people improve their mental health.

Key Assumptions

However, despite the variety of approaches, counselling is built on a foundation of key assumptions, factors that need to be in place before good work can be completed. These are:

- o   High-quality relationship.
- o   Non-directive approach.
- o   Safe sanctuary.

High-Quality Relationship

The quality of the relationship between the therapist and the client is a critically-important variable in successful outcomes. Indeed, the depth of the relationship is seen to be more potent than the specific techniques deployed. Carl Rogers, the founder of person-centred counselling, described this as follows:

> ... our sharply different therapists achieve good results in quite different ways. For one, an impatient, no-nonsense, let's put-the-cards-on-the-table approach is most effective, because in such an approach he is most openly being himself. For another, it may be a much more gentle and more obviously warm approach, because this is the way the therapist is (Rogers, 1967: 185-186).

This high-quality relationship idea is mirrored in coaching:

> Regardless of preferred theoretical perspective, the foundation of effective coaching is the successful formation of a collaborative relationship (Stober & Grant, 2006: 360).

Non-Directive Approach

A key assumption in therapy is that the solution resides inside each client. The therapist doesn't supply the answer but facilitates a process where the answer emerges from the client. Regardless of the presenting issue, everyone can work it out.

Across all therapeutic approaches (including psychiatry), the goal of remaining non-directive is continually stressed, with the client seen as the central actor:

... you cannot tell people how to live their lives. They make choices. If they want to get better, they probably will and, if they want to create more problems for themselves, they will (Browne, 2008: 117).

The work of Chris Argyris in the field of Organisation Development offers a parallel here. He developed the concept of single-loop and double-loop learning. Single-loop learning refers to an organisation's ability to problem-solve and overcome challenges. Double-loop learning (much less in evidence) is the ability to problem-prevent, learning from the environment and past experiences through *post mortems* (1990). The underpinning rationale in therapy is very similar. The goal is for the client to develop a 'double-loop' ability, resolving future problems using their own resources. While being non-directive seems like a relatively straightforward instruction, the pressure on therapists to tell someone what to do can be intense, sometimes emanating directly from clients. Shainberg illustrates this brilliantly:

> Often patients do not know clearly what they want, think or feel. They do not feel they can create their own fates from within. They are dependant on others for self-esteem and direction. They can bear minimal anxiety, have little patience. They experience little connection to having caused their own difficulties. They disrupt the relationship when they are not treated in the way they expect or when results that they want are not forthcoming. All this makes for a difficult person to be with ... the patient conveying 'Help me. Do something to make my life better. If you don't you are incompetent or ungiving. I will hate you or leave or lose respect for you' (1985: 174).

Pressure to instruct the client can also be driven by unconscious forces:

> ... if the story is a negative one and the client has little optimism about being able to improve or change their situation, then you can get dragged down into a sense of hopelessness. This can then set off the following sorts of reaction in the coach; a desire

to fix things, an urgency to get a result ... or a feeling of helplessness and inadequacy (Pelham, 2014: 35).

There is an enormous crossover with coaching under this heading. While the coaching process assumes an 'appetite for change', it can't be externally imposed. The coachee's motivation to engage and their self-discipline in following improvement steps determine the outcome. A coach can encourage, but ultimately changes must be embraced by the coachee (Witherspoon & White, 1996).

Safe Sanctuary

Counselling provides a sanctuary for clients to explore troubling thoughts. Branches of therapy that place particular emphasis on attachment theory (importance of early childhood experiences with the primary caregiver) see this aspect as being especially important:

> The presence of a sufficient safe haven provides a child with a
> sense of a secure base from which to increasingly and
> confidently explore the world – and to which he or she can
> return as needed as part of ever-widening circles. This is
> important for development because, as researchers have noted,
> the more threatened an individual feels, 'the more primitive' (or
> regressed) becomes the style of the thinking and behaviour
> (Perry *et al*, 1995: 274).

Attachment theory suggests that many people cling to their parent (or other authority figures later in life) rather than face the separation distress necessary for the development of a healthy ego (Drake, 2009: 5). Indeed, counselling can be conceptualised as a relationship in which the professional becomes a surrogate attachment figure, allowing experiences the client's original attachment figures could not make room for (*op cit*, 14). While this is useful background material for the professional, it's seldom shared directly with the client. Telling a seasoned executive that you are playing the role of surrogate father is probably not the smartest intervention! The safe sanctuary idea is communicated by remaining non-judgemental and through the unconditional positive regard stance described earlier. This allows the client to contain anxiety and, sometimes, to make sense of contradictions:

You are there to 'hold your client's feet to the fire', not to fan the flames, nor to put the fire out, nor to press the client to accept the organisation's view, nor to allow your client to run away into self-deception (McMahon & Archer, 2010: 50-51).

Case Study D: Unconditional Positive Regard

Working on an international assignment, I was coaching a mid-level executive. Thirty minutes in, it seemed as if we were reliving an earlier session. I had a strong sense of *déjà vu*. This manager continually outsourced the blame for his lack of career success. His ability hadn't been fully recognised. He was dealing with a very difficult group that couldn't be managed. The person who'd been promoted ahead of him had inferior skills and so on. I found my attention wandering away from the client onto other unrelated matters.

But the following thoughts kept pulling me back into the session:

o What is there to really like about this client?

o How can I demonstrate that I value working with him and am able to support him?

o How can I understand and accept the world from his perspective and stop being judgmental and inwardly critical of his views?

While all of this was unspoken, forcing my attention back onto the client had the following impact. He began to open up, to question some of his own assumptions, to verbally test ideas about how he might more successfully manage relationships going forward. All I'd done was to mentally 'come back into the room'. Somehow, that was communicated and that was all that was required. While it took a bit of time, he eventually worked out the solution himself.

Change Difficulty

Let's assume that a high-quality relationship is established, the style of the counsellor is non-directive and the client feels that he is in a safe, non-judgemental sanctuary. Does this guarantee change – that is, the presenting issues will disappear if these three conditions are met? Not necessarily. Kegan & Lahey in their influential book, *Immunity to Change*, demonstrate how difficult it is to effect change, using case examples from medicine to underscore their argument (2009). For example, when patients facing a major health risk are told by doctors to change their lifestyle – for example, go on a diet or quit smoking – only about one in seven actually follow through. If life and death matters provoke a response in only *circa* 14% of people, it's little wonder that shifts in behaviour for non-life-threatening issues are difficult. In one study, they researched the number of patients who stopped taking post-stroke medication (57% had quit). In this scenario the medication would have prevented them getting a future stroke, there were no side effects and the costs were covered by Medicaid.

Their central argument is that we have an immune system that keeps us safe from the anxiety of changing (Kegan & Lahey, 2001). While anxiety may seem like the mental equivalent of the common cold (everyone feels anxiety at times), the power of this unconscious process should not be underestimated. Having an in-built anxiety management system allows us to feel safe. That's the upside. The downside is that it stops us stretching beyond what's comfortable and creates a false belief that certain things are impossible. A client may be following a life script (from Transactional Analysis), parental messages written long ago that exercise huge power in shaping a child. These messages are normally of two types:

- o Attributions – she is clever / clumsy / assertive / cheeky.
- o Injunctions – powerful statements of how not to be – for example, "don't ever speak back to your father again".

Once these attributions and injunctions are accepted, we keep ploughing the same furrow, over and over again. The researchers describe this as follows: If 14 frogs sat on a log and three decided to jump in a lake, how many would be left? 11? No, 14. There's a difference between deciding to do something and actually doing it, a chasm between desire and action (Kegan & Lahey, *op cit*).

Counsellors (and coaches) bump up directly against this 'immunity to change' all the time. For example, following the administration of a 360^0 feedback exercise, it's not uncommon for an executive to announce "There's nothing new for me in this". Here the executive has been reminded (again) of things that people dislike but she decided not to (or simply couldn't) change.

To understand why seemingly smart people sabotage their careers in this way, we need an insight into what's happening beneath our conscious awareness.

Making Changes Stick

In working with clients and coachees, respondents in this research stated that the core difficulty is seldom about identifying what needs to be done (target-setting); the difficulty is more often around making new thinking or behaviour patterns stick. Many times in my own practice I've seen that it's easy to change people's mood through active listening and responding in an empathic way. Yet, it's much more difficult to get people to change underlying thinking patterns or behaviour.

Why? Because a fear of changing is often buried deep:

> You can see the very good reason why you are holding yourself
> back: you want to save your life as you know it (Kegan &
> Lahey, 2009: 253).

On first glance this idea seems counter-intuitive, almost unbelievable. People come to coaching and counselling to improve aspects of their life. Why would they subsequently not change when they've outwardly signed-up for this? Counsellors who have trained from a psychodynamic perspective argue that unconscious anxiety essentially puts a brake on change:

> The true reason that we find change so difficult is that we have
> developed and perfected any number of defensive tactics to keep
> us exactly as we are. These are defences against anxiety and we
> all have them, even those well-functioning, stable and highly
> successful people in senior roles in organisations who appear in
> our lives as clients (Rogers, 2011: 5).

One respondent commented:

> People can get addicted to their own misery. It becomes a way
> of life. At least they know that game (Purchaser A).

There was an amusing illustration of this in the movie, *Annie Hall*.
Two women were talking and one said, "The food here is terrible".
Her friend replied, "Yes, and the portions are so small".

To help break these historical chains, some clients search for a
deeper meaning in life. Explaining this, one respondent said:

> Sometimes clients lock onto Jesus. I'm OK with that. Christ is
> less harmful than heroin (Therapist Q).

Change stirs up anxiety, by challenging our established patterns.
Resistance to change therefore makes perfect sense when viewed as a
mechanism designed to lower anxiety. This issue cannot be
understood or addressed without a deep knowledge of psychology /
human development principles. For example, Kegan suggests that the
core role of the coach or counsellor is "building psychological muscle"
(1998), which goes well beyond teaching. If these underlying defence
mechanisms are not understood, the client's problem thinking or
behaviour will resurface and any changes effected will be short-lived.
These deeper ideas are extracted in counselling, brought to the
surface and explored by the client. The paradoxical theory of change
holds that in order to make a transition from A to B, the client must
fully engage with and understand A (Beisser, 1970). In therapy, the
focus on the individual's psychological development requires an
understanding of their 'mental tapes'. In contrast, the coaching role is
directed at getting movement, essentially to do enough psychology to
uncover anything that's blocking progress, but no more than this:
"It's not excavation for excavation's sake" (Therapist U). Of course,
the assumption here is that the coach knows enough psychology to
understand this distinction.

Discovering Patterns

Catherine Sandler, the author of an influential textbook on executive
coaching, describes her approach as follows:

> I draw on multiple perspectives to understand my clients but at
> the heart of my practice lies the psychodynamic approach ...
> ideas about the human mind that have their roots in the ground-
> breaking theories of Sigmund Freud, the founder of
> psychoanalysis (Sandler, 2012).

Her argument is that many of the techniques developed in psychotherapy have direct application to the coaching field; they shed light on unconscious thoughts and feelings, invisible drivers of long-established patterns of behaviour, an idea supported by extensive research (Beebe & Lachmann, 2002). One of Freud's key insights was that people have a strong unconscious tendency to retain patterns over their lifetime, a template for behaviour that's continually re-cycled, in line with the notion that the "child is psychologically the father of the man or the woman" (Nelson-Jones, 2000: 41). Like railway tracks, we continually follow the same routes, even where the results are negative (Sandler, 2011: 17). The payoff (behaviour always has a psychological payoff) is the security that comes from familiarity.

Here again we touch on this centrally-important yet troubling issue. Why would someone choose to continue a 'negative pattern'? If you booked a holiday to Athens but didn't enjoy it, you wouldn't return the following year. So why do we allow negative patterns to continue in our lives?

The answer is that these processes are mostly hidden from view, outside of our conscious awareness. We don't instruct our lungs to keep breathing, it happens automatically. Similarly, unconscious thought processes operate on automatic pilot. Psychodynamic theory posits that we develop defences early in life in our relationships with key figures (parents and others). This combines with our innate temperament to produce an overall way of being. As we develop and mature, these defences may moderate and become flexible. However, people can find it very difficult to break patterns, even when these are no longer helpful or may even be dysfunctional.

Step one is to unearth these patterns. Step two is to explore them. Step three is to change (if the client decides to change).

Mental Health

'Reality TV' has helped to bring mental health problems to a wider audience. For example, there's been a recent upsurge in TV programmes focusing on the addictive patterns of hoarders, where it becomes unsafe to live in a house that has so much stuff. On one level, buying and storing huge amounts of material – old newspapers or food – seems nonsensical. While spouses and children of hoarders argue this rationally, they don't recognise that the hoarder is gripped by an unconscious process that won't allow them to change; not having clutter makes them terribly anxious. Until the underlying pattern is understood, there is no behavioural change. As Pelham argues:

> We are, in fact, seeking to loosen the grip of the system of self-regulation so that something new can happen (*op cit*: 6).

It's only when the invisible is made visible that it can be worked on. Coaches who don't work in this therapeutic way limit their range – to teaching or developing tactics to overcome short-term problems.

Without understanding these underlying processes, which are essentially designed to keep us as we are, it's not possible to do transformational work. Supporting this 'change is difficult' thesis, the psychiatrist Ivor Browne put forward the following explanation:

> Even at its simplest, any change involves two things – work and suffering. The deeper the change to be accomplished, the greater the amount of work, pain and suffering involved. People resist change for this very reason, even when they realise that change will have a positive benefit (Browne, 2008: 259).

The pain of where the client is today must outweigh the pain they will inevitably experience in moving towards a better tomorrow. The process isn't easy; not everyone will embark and not everyone who does will complete the journey.

Considering Transference

Transference and counter-transference provide a further example of a concept that emerged in counselling but has since migrated and has become a centrally-important idea in therapeutic coaching.

While a full discussion of transference is outside of our scope, the way in which a coachee perceives and interacts with the coach may reflect their interactions with significant parental or authority figures in the past. Counter-transference is the term used to describe the coach's reaction to the coachee, essentially: *How does this person make me feel?*

The central question for both coaches and counsellors is "Am I working on **their** stuff or on **my** stuff?". For example, some counsellors over-identify with the client and want to 'rescue them' – perhaps fulfilling an unconscious need they have within themselves to play this role. One respondent described their *modus operandi*:

> Our fundamental philosophy is to impress on clients that they
> need to take responsibility for their own lives. If a counsellor is
> spending too much time with a client, a key question is whether
> the ownership of the problem has become unclear (Therapist F).

Transference happens in all human interactions and impacts the extent to which a relationship can be successful. Knowing how these processes work is of huge value to both coaches and counsellors (adding considerable weight to the idea that training in psychology is needed by coaches).

The conceptual diagram overleaf seeks to represent a continuum of support and the overlap that exists between the various coaching and counselling approaches.

Boundary Line

Having considered both coaching and counselling separately, we now tackle the central question: *Can the boundary that separates coaching from counselling be drawn with precision?*

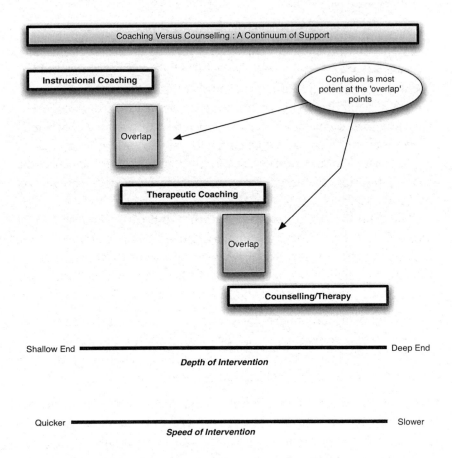

In order to address this, we pose six fundamental questions:

- o **Question #1:** Do coaching / counselling 'professionals' differ?
- o **Question #2:** Are coachees and clients different?
- o **Question #3:** In coaching, is the primary customer the coachee or the organisation?
- o **Question #4:** Are the core processes different?
- o **Question #5:** Is the engagement style different between coaches and counsellors?
- o **Question #6:** How do organisations choose the perfect coach or counsellor?

COACHING *VERSUS* COUNSELLING

QUESTION #1: DO THE PROFESSIONALS DIFFER?

At this moment in time, there is no difference between the two professions around *licensing* requirements. Anyone can use the 'coach' label and there's a worldwide industry offering a range of certification programmes. Similarly, anyone can market themselves as a 'counsellor'. While all of the respondents in this research were qualified (in coaching, counselling, psychology or psychotherapy), it turns out that there's no legislation in Ireland that outlaws the use of the labels *coach*, *counsellor* or *therapist*. Unlike lawyers or medical doctors, anyone can claim to be a counsellor without completing formal training.

While the coaches met during this research were *qualified* (both as university graduates and also as coaches), they were not drawn from a single discipline. Coaches emerge from the ranks of HR professionals and executives across all functions, a finding mirrored in the research literature.

One major study (surveying 2,529 professional coaches) demonstrated the wide variety of backgrounds: consultants (40.8%), managers (30.8%), executives (30.2%), teachers (15.7%) and salespeople (13.8%). Interestingly, only 4.8% of respondents were trained psychologists (Grant & Cavanagh, 2004).[8]

Other researchers have identified law and sports as additional training grounds for executive coaches (Brotman *et al*, 1998; Kilburg, 1996).

---

[8] The total is greater than 100% as there is some overlap and double-counting.

Joining Rationale

Respondents in this research moved into coaching and counselling for a variety of reasons. Most had 'grey hair', having come from some other profession (the average age of the coaches in the survey group was 45+). This finding mirrors international practice.

In one study executive coaches averaged 24+ years' work experience (Judge & Cowell, 1997). Some coaches were retired, operating part-time to extend their working life. Some were *downshifters*, people who valued self-employment on the basis of having more control over their working life. Some had signed-up, driven primarily by personal interest:

> I got into the game for self-development, a sort of DIY approach to therapy. We are all endlessly fascinated by our own psychology. By learning how to support others, I was really learning how to support myself (Coach G).

> As a senior HR Manager, I noticed that leaders were often blocked, not so much by their technical capabilities, but by a lack of awareness or self-limiting beliefs or behaviour. I wanted to understand why and how I could help (Therapist T).

> I studied psychology at university and spotted coaching as an interest early on. The university stuff was academic, a bit too dry, so I moved into practice. Non-drug approaches to psychiatric illness, that's what really interests me (Therapist U).

Coaching Affiliations

While *learning the coaching game* was seen as important, the issue of continuous professional development (CPD) was deemed less critical by the coaches interviewed. Almost 50% of this group were affiliated to a formal coaching body, but a much smaller number were involved in ongoing professional education. All of the respondents were qualified as coaches, some having completed significant training.

Several programmes were formally *recognised* by a coaching body – for example, the University of Strathclyde program is accredited by the International Coach Federation. Other coaches were focused on acquiring the 'badge' of a respected university. The high levels of training supports the earlier arguments made about the growing professionalism of coaching, albeit the CPD issue is 'patchy'.

Regulated Coaching

Given the potential impact that coaches have on people's lives, there's a strong argument for a professional body to set and monitor standards. The concern is that inappropriately trained coaches will conduct atheoretical interventions and may even harm coachees, particularly those who present with mental health problems (Naughton, 2002; Cavanagh, 2005).

Of course, having a central governing body doesn't *guarantee* high standards or continuing professional development. I have been a member of the Chartered Institute of Personnel and Development for 30+ years. During all of that time, to the best of my recollection, only once have members been asked to submit evidence of continuous professional development (a suggestion that was later quietly abandoned). However, people cannot become members of the CIPD until they complete the baseline training or have significant experience, so membership at least ensures common *entry standards*.

A regulatory coaching body would set minimum entry standards and could have *teeth* – the ability to enforce sanctions, ensure CPD and remove members from the register for proven malpractice, essentially *policing* the profession.

Psychologically Trained?

A key question raised above is whether coaches should be trained in psychology and, if so, to what depth? The short answer to this question is *yes* – at least to the standard of conscious incompetence – that is, *being aware of what they don't know* (Kneebone *et al*, 2002). An analogy here is with people who work with teenagers being made aware of suicide ideation. While they may not know how to *treat* this, they need to recognise the symptoms.

In similar vein, coaches need to know when to refer coachees onto someone else, asking "Is this a manager with a problem (coaching client) or a 'problem manager' (counselling client)?". Cavanagh suggests the following indicators:

- o If the coachee has been experiencing distress / dysfunction for an extended period.
- o Extreme behaviours that are pervasive.
- o Client defensiveness and resistance to change (2005: 23).

The following table (modified from the original by Buckley & Buckley (2006: 78) provides guidelines on the *when to refer* dilemma.

Continue Coaching or Refer to Counselling?		
Element	Consider Continuing	Consider Stopping
Issue is *separate* from the coaching focus or context	Coachee's problems seem separate from the coaching context.	Problems seem pervasive or immediately threatening – for example, unable to experience pleasure, increase in hopelessness or helplessness (depression), acute anxiety. Evidence of physical / emotional abuse. Mention of suicide.
Issue is *temporary*, likely to resolve itself in a couple of weeks	Temporary issue.	Long-term or recurring – for example, poor sleep patterns, exhaustion, hyper-active, substance abuse.
Issue will be appropriately supported *elsewhere*	Coachee is well-supported elsewhere.	Coaching is not focused on emotional support or coachee has little external support.
Coachee is emotionally robust / *resilient*	Coachee is a strong person who can normally cope with psychological pain.	Coachee is an emotionally fragile person may struggle – for example, irritability, anger outbursts, continually crying.
Coachee is *self-aware* around this issue	Coachee shows high self-awareness on this topic.	Low self-awareness – for example, denies the issue or seems unaware of it. Unable to focus, intrusive thoughts.
Coachee has a *plan* to deal with this issue	The plan is realistic and positive.	No plan exists or the plan is negative – for example, self-harm or preoccupation with death.

Continue Coaching or Refer to Counselling?		
Element	Consider Continuing	Consider Stopping
Issue is something that may *impact on the coach*	Coach is fully aware of counter-transference issues.	Not aware of counter-transference or uncomfortable in being able to deal with this.

As part of the research, I tried to determine how often coachees are referred for counselling. When this happens, do people take a twin-track approach? A couple of practical barriers were highlighted:

> Coachees react negatively to being told that they need to see a therapist. It's delicate, as if you've already made a determination that they have some form of mental illness (Coach R).

The general consensus was that it is very difficult to pursue both streams at the same time:

> You only have so much headspace. People can attend coaching or counselling, but not both (Coach J).

In practice, while it was not possible to determine the 'rate of referral', anecdotally this seemed quite low (movement in the opposite direction is also possible – for example, a client moving from therapy to coaching).

Beyond Referrals

My considered view is that psychological training for coaches needs to go beyond recognising when to refer people for counselling. This is similar to the argument put forward by Barrett-Leonard:

> There can be no openness to the client's experience if there is no openness to one's own experience. And without openness there can be no empathy either (1962: 4).

Without personal insight, coaches are limited to making *surface interventions*, when the needs of the client may require a deeper excavation. Pelham suggests why some coaches steer away from this:

> Many people coming into coaching have not undertaken in-depth personal development processes such as therapy and counselling. They imagine that, if they take the lid off their own material, they might be overwhelmed (Pelham, 2014: 26).

There is a subtle but important issue at play here. Arguably, clients who present for therapy have specific symptoms and an expectation of *treatment*, whereas coachees who are wrestling with similar mental health issues may not even recognise this. It follows that coaches need finely-tuned diagnostic skills and the ability to consider psychopathological issues side by side with offering the more goal-focused relationship that typically characterises coaching (Grant, 2008: 33).

Case Study E: Troubled Coachee

I was asked to intervene in a long-running dispute between an employee, her union and the employer. To kickstart the process, I met the staff member in the union offices. She seemed quite normal and the conversation was somewhat low-key. For the first hour or so, we spoke about a number of 'incidents' in the employing organisation, which she felt were *annoying*. While these were certainly examples of poor management practice, none seemed particularly egregious.

Then the conversation took an unusual turn. As she became more comfortable, the employee disclosed a range of bizarre incidents. For example, she believed the company was monitoring her by sending 'radio wave' signals to control her thought processes and also was having her followed at weekends.

I knew the employer of old, having dealt with them on a number of previous occasions. While all organisations suffer from 'managerial lapses', I was confident that the suggested incidents hadn't happened (the company was adamant that no form of personal surveillance was in place).

Eventually, we referred this employee to the psychiatric services. It transpired that she was suffering from acute paranoia and had to be treated on an in-patient basis.

While almost all coaches would *refer* a similar client, the dilemma is that the issues are seldom as clear-cut as in this case. It's probably best to conceptualise *mental illness* as aspects of thinking or behaviour that lie along a continuum, rather than a discrete 'have or have not' condition (Buckley & Buckley, 2006: 15).

Best Background

Some scholars argue that psychologists make the best coaches and that it may even be *dangerous* to allow coaches who don't have this background to practice. Berglas picks up this thread:

> I believe that in an alarming number of situations, executive coaches who lack rigorous psychological training do more harm than good. By dint of their backgrounds and biases, they downplay or simply ignore deep-seated psychological problems they don't understand (2002).

Not everyone agrees. Arguing against the incursion of *counselling* techniques, Peltier suggests:

> The talking cure ... is too slow, too personal, it provides no guarantees, and it lacks the punch and focus demanded by those in the fast lane (2001, XVI).

At one end of the spectrum, some coaches are trained psychologists / psychotherapists and this may have been their singular role since leaving university. Coaching has emerged in recent years as a new sub-speciality of psychology (Peltier, 2009) and some people are attracted to *positive psychology*, as distinct from working with psychological dysfunction more often associated with clinical roles (Naughton, 2002). Half a century ago, Abraham Maslow argued:

> The science of psychology has been far more successful on the negative than on the positive side. It has revealed to us much about man's shortcomings, his illness, his sins, but little about potentialities, his virtues, his achievable aspirations, or his full psychological height. It is as if psychology has voluntarily restricted itself to only half its rightful jurisdiction, and that, the darker, meaner half (Maslow, 1954: 354).

At the other end of the spectrum, there are coaches who have never studied psychology. These people typically bring strong business expertise and may have tacit knowledge – for example, about the oil exploration industry. Holding the *centre* position are business coaches who have received *some* psychological training. The argument put forward by Berglas presupposes that, as the presenting issues are typically *psychological* in nature, psychologists perform best as coaches. Yet, a psychologist who has never worked in a multinational company may find it difficult to understand the pressures of dealing with interorganisation politics or to guide a client in plotting a career trajectory.

Lee makes the point that coaches who come with a strong psychological background but lack knowledge of the corporate world tend to turn coaching into therapy. Conversely, coaches who are steeped in the corporate world but who lack psychological-mindedness, focus on short-term problem-solving and fail to unearth deeper issues (2003).

Who Performs Best?

Part of the problem in coming to a definitive view on *who performs best* (psychologists *versus* non-psychologists) is that there is as much difference *within* psychology / counselling in terms of approach, as there is *between* coaching and counselling. The personal style of the individual (for example, the ability to establish deep relationships) seems as important as any particular training, with one proviso. This research suggests that great coaching can be done by people who are not formally-trained psychologists – provided they have received *enough* psychological training (including working on *themselves*) to uncover the issues brought forward by clients. Without this, there's a limitation to what can be achieved. Lietaer captures this neatly by asserting:

> The therapist can never bring the client further than where he is himself as a person (1993: 23).

One argument is that psychologists already possess a large number of the skills needed to provide executive coaching and therefore are the most *qualified* service providers (Sperry, 1993; Kilburg, 1996;

Brotman *et al*, 1998). Psychologists are qualified to define what's required when behaviour change is the desired outcome based on an understanding of psychometric tests, cognitive styles, motivation and so forth.

Kilburg (1997) lists a number of skills psychologists possess that make them qualified to provide executive coaching services – including the ability to listen, empathise, provide feedback, challenge and explore the executive's world. He later (2000) argued that, although one does not necessarily have to be a psychologist to provide executive coaching, having psychoanalytic knowledge (possessed by some but not all psychologists) enhances the results.

While the importance of the baseline knowledge is accepted, many of the skills listed (for example, an ability to empathise) are certainly not confined to psychologists. Further, an awareness of business management, organisation politics and leadership are often necessary elements in the mix (Kiel *et al*, 1996; Levinson, 1996; Saporito, 1996; Harris, 1999).

Overall, it's very difficult to make a case that an 'ideal coach' comes from any particular discipline. There are simply too many variables.

Horses for Courses

Liljenstrand & Nebeker (2008) surveyed over 2,000 coaches and found a significant overlap between academic backgrounds and client goals, suggesting that coaches from different disciplines are hired to accomplish specific objectives. For example, they discovered that coaches with *business backgrounds* were hired more often when coaching focused on task skills (for example, sales). Coaches with a psychology background were hired when engagements focused on interpersonal skills. Outwardly, this *'horses for courses'* argument seems like a reasonable proposition – coaching is likely to be more 'successful' when there is a *fit* between the coach and the coaching objectives. However, this view places a heavy emphasis on the 'content role' of coaching (in line with the instructional coaching model described earlier). In therapeutic coaching, where the core assumption is that the 'answer' resides *within* the client, content knowledge is deemed much less important. Overall, there's no simple or 'neat' answer under this heading.

Training Coaches

As coaching evolves, there's a growing recognition of the importance of psychology. Indeed, some senior coaches migrate from a formal counselling background (for example, Catherine Sandler, one of the current *high priests* in the profession, holds a Ph.D. in counselling psychology).

Central Point

Therapeutic coaching is not something that can be learned over a long-weekend. Arguably, it's easier for a trained counsellor to *make the switch* and work as a coach as the *training period* in counselling is much longer and those who have published, teach or lead professional associations (thought leaders) colour the thinking of newer coaches entering the profession, many of whom do not share this therapy background.

The problem is that thought leaders are not easy to emulate. For example, not every coach shares the academic background (Ph.D.) and depth of training of Geoff Pelham who leads the UCD coach training programme. Trying to emulate Geoff's coaching style is like a beginner entering a life drawing competition against Michelangelo. While, of course, any technique can be learned if enough time is invested, the question is how *accessible* these ideas are to *normal* coaches? Sandler, recognising this point, states:

> Using this model requires an unusual degree of self-awareness and sensitivity to the full range of conscious and unconscious emotions (2012).

The range of ideas *imported* from counselling undoubtedly can be helpful in providing insight into the human condition with benefits for coaches in having access to these concepts. Yet, the question remains whether these techniques can actually be applied? If coaches cannot use these ideas without significant training, are they better to steer clear of therapeutic coaching altogether? Is a *little bit of knowledge,* on the part of the professional, a *dangerous thing* for the coachee?

What Training?

Psychological training in an academic sense doesn't necessarily lead to the development of psychological-mindedness. There may be little of no *awareness development* in psychology students, even those who become skilled in terms of 'tool usage' – for example, occupational psychologists trained to interpret psychometrics. To overstate the point, smart sociopaths can achieve a 'first' in psychology exams.

The core argument here is that the *personal development* of the coach is as important as *theory* and *skill* development (Pelham, 2014: 29). In recognition of this, therapists are steeped in the tradition of doing *personal work* – they are on the receiving end of a specified number of personal therapy hours. In similar vein, coaches need significant exposure to personal therapy to avoid:

> ... artificial translations of clinical theory ... insufficiently complex to help create a sustainable change (Stojnov & Pavlovic, 2010: 138).

In short, coaches need the required skills to *operationalise* the therapeutic model. Being aware that particular concepts *exist* is not enough; in-depth training makes these ideas *useable*. The most obvious method to develop psychological awareness is to undertake personal counselling, either one-on-one or in a group context *(emotional intelligence learning laboratories)*. The purpose is not simply to understand yourself better – becoming more self-aware – but also to understand and appreciate others.

Training Facilities

A couple of years ago, I visited Regis University in Denver, Colorado, where psychotherapy / counselling forms a core part of the curriculum. The university has built a series of rooms fitted with full sound and TV recording and equipped these with two-way mirrors. This enables coaching / counselling sessions to be witnessed 'live' and recorded as future training inputs. Clients are fully aware of this. It gives them access to professionals whom they might not otherwise be able to afford (sessions are run *pro bono* or on a reduced cost basis).

At this point in time, no equivalent facility exists in Ireland. The construction of a similar facility would offer an additional benefit. Despite the fact that the various coaching and counselling theories are well-known (through published books and articles), they are less often *demonstrated*. While materials are available on the Internet, the categorisation is piecemeal and difficult to source. Best practice video demonstrations of the various coaching (and counselling) *approaches* would *paint a thousand words,* making these concepts easier to understand and assimilate.

In the coaching arena, there's no 'easy answer' to the question *Who performs best?* While psychologists and business leaders bring different skills to the table, the orientation of the professional seems at least as important as any particular background or training. While therapists typically study counselling / psychology and business coaches study business (plus coaching), there's no evidence from this research that either group provides 'higher order' support.

QUESTION #2: ARE COACHEES AND CLIENTS DIFFERENT?

One possible way to differentiate coaching from counselling is on the basis of the *type* of client. An implicit suggestion across much of the counselling and coaching literature is that different approaches should be taken with *clinical* and *non-clinical* populations. We've shown earlier that psychology has primarily focused on the amelioration of *dysfunction*, helping clients who present in distress. While there are many ways to categorise mental illness, it can be labelled as *"a personal construction used repeatedly in spite of consistent invalidation"* – in other words, a refusal or inability to face objective facts (Kelly, 1991: 193). In contrast, coaching tends to be more future-focused and coachees are seen to come from a *normal* – that is, mentally healthy – population (Grant, 2003). As coachees are *psychologically resilient*, they are supposedly more open to challenge than people who attend counselling.

Positive Psychology and the Non-Clinical Population

Extending this outwards, there is a wider debate within the counselling profession around what's come to be labelled as 'positive psychology', which focuses on human potential rather than psychological dysfunction (Seligman & Csikszentmihalyi, 2000; Snyder & McCullough, 2000):

> In working with individuals to improve the quality of their lives, psychology has traditionally focused on alleviating dysfunctionality or treating psychopathology in clinical or counselling populations rather than enhancing the life experience of normal adult populations (Grant, 2003: 253).

This has been articulated as a movement *beyond the zero point* - returning people to zero on a figurative minus-10 to a plus-10 scale of mental health (Peterson, 2000). The movement towards positive psychology is a recognition that the profession has largely ignored two of its three *missions*:

o Curing mental illness.

o Helping all people to lead more productive lives.

o Identifying and nurturing talent (Linley & Harrington, 2008: 42-43).

A further strand can be identified in this argument. Van Velsor & Guthrie (1998) suggest that a number of variables make executives *more receptive* to coaching – for example, the ability to recognize ineffective behaviours and identify opportunities for learning new skills. Particular personality traits (for example, high self-esteem) positively influence the ability to learn from developmental experiences. On a broadly similar tack, London (2002) and Goleman (2007) suggest that a high feedback orientation and emotional intelligence, respectively, may influence the extent to which a client is able to benefit from a professional relationship. The implicit argument here is that 'service users' for coaching and counselling are fundamentally different.

Incorrect Assumptions

Only a novice in this area would accept the argument that coaching and counselling populations can be neatly separated in this way.

On the counselling side, if someone decides to improve the quality of their emotional life by attending, does that signify dysfunction or mental health?

In coaching, my experience suggests that there is no *typical* client. It's incorrect and can actually be unhelpful to view all coaching clients as mentally robust and open to *challenge*, even people who occupy very senior roles. Sometimes CEOs spend their lives in organisations where they receive falsely positive feedback from staff, which actually makes them *less* rather than *more* robust (Mooney, 2009). Robustness is *person-* rather than *category*-dependent, with the overall rider that the intervention depth (by coaches or counsellors) should always be dictated by *field conditions* (Mackewn, 1997). Lukaszewski (1988) suggested that an inability to access people who *"ask questions, provide advice and give counsel"* poses a severe hurdle for many senior executives. Most people working closely with senior executives are afraid (or don't know how) to confront their behaviour, territory which is the *heartland* for executive coaches.

For sure, working in a *deep way* requires someone open to the challenge of grappling with complex and sometimes paradoxical issues (Spinelli & Horner, 2008). However, people with these traits come from all walks of life. The assertion that executives have superior insight or higher emotional intelligence than non-executives is so flimsy that it hardly merits a rebuttal. The number of executives who *are forced to leave* organisations provides evidence that this population is not automatically *mentally healthy*. Studies using different methodologies, in different organisations and across national cultures, illustrate that failed managers exercise poor judgment, have troubled relationships, don't build teams and can't manage themselves or learn from their mistakes (Executive Tripwires: www.tandemconsulting.ie). Further, counselling clients present *voluntarily* for support, while a percentage of executive coachees are *sent* for coaching by the employer – they don't *automatically* have more self-insight. A final point under this heading is that the stress of senior leadership roles makes the need for support *more* rather than *less* likely. Indeed, it raises an intriguing possibility around the *stigma* normally associated with counselling:

> Although coaching is aimed at non-clinical populations it may
> be that some individuals seek coaching as a more socially-
> acceptable form of therapy (Grant, 2008: 26).

While some mental health issues would make it virtually impossible to sustain an executive role, the assumption that executives are automatically *high-functioning* seems shaky at best and a distortion at worst.

Life *versus* Work

One suggested split between coaching and counselling is along the *work* and *non-work* dimensions in a manager's life. Coaching is supposedly directed towards work-related issues – for example, how to manage a difficult employee or prepare a strategic plan. In contrast, counselling is seen to be a useful method to support a staff member who was 'not coping' with general life issues – for example, stress, marriage breakdown, alcoholism or bereavement (Purchaser B). While this argument certainly offers a *neat* distinction, it has no basis in fact. Coachees often *present* with work-related issues, but later decide to work on personal stuff. Equally, people who present for counselling often want to 'fix' work-related issues (Therapist T; Coach G).

Based on this research, there is no evidence to support the idea that coaching and counselling can be separated along the lines that 'service users' differ. It is judgmental and inaccurate to label all *coachees* as mentally healthy and suggest that all *clients* are the opposite. Consider the following definition:

> Counseling can be defined as a relatively short-term,
> interpersonal, theory-based process of helping persons who are
> basically psychologically healthy, resolve developmental and
> situational problems (American Counseling Association, 2007).

Most of us experience episodes in our lives when we would benefit from the support of a trained and sympathetic guide.

Kahn reinforces this point when he argues that the myth in psychotherapy is that in each session there is one distressed person with problems and one professional who has it all together (1997, 125). The 'split' of people into two populations – those who are 'mentally well' and those who are 'mentally unwell' – is a false dichotomy. Closer to home, the psychiatrist Ivor Browne made the following observation:

> When I joined the staff of St. Brendan's there were some very
> strange doctors working there. They certainly fitted the old
> saying that 'the only difference between the doctors and patients
> in a mental hospital was that some of the patients changed'
> (Browne, 2008: 101).

QUESTION #3: WHO IS THE PRIMARY CUSTOMER?

When coaching is arranged and funded by the employer, who is the client? Is the *primary customer* the executive or the organisation? When conflicts arise, what needs take precedence? Do boundaries around confidential and non-confidential information exist, zones of privacy that cannot be breached simply because the organisation is stumping up the funding?

None of these issues arise when counselling fees are paid directly by the client.

Respecting Boundaries

Protecting confidentiality has potential to create a number of difficulties and coaches need to tread carefully in this space.

An analogy here is with child psychologists. While they typically give the parents of a patient information on progress, parents are not allowed to have complete and total access to the child's every word simply because they pay the bills (Feldman & Lankau, 2005). In coaching, if someone *does not want to change* or expresses the view that the *problem* is with the organisation (not themselves), how should the coach respond?

Some of the potential conflicts under this heading are addressed when the coach has a defined ethical stance that's communicated to all parties at the contracting stage. This *respecting boundaries* idea was borne out by the field research. In practice, most of the *buyers* are HR professionals. Provided that the coach makes *what's discussible* and *what's not* crystal clear, they are happy to work within boundary constraints. A good example of this is the development of a coaching plan.

Practice Difference: Coaching Plan

The development of coaching plans is one area that provides *clear blue water* between coaching and counselling. It has been widely recommended that executive coaching should have clear objectives with goals understood and agreed at the outset (Valerio & Lee, 2005). A coaching plan typically lays out the core *purpose* of the intervention. Without this, Sandler argues:

> ... the coaching relationship becomes a cosy twosome, more-or-less detached from the organisation that is funding the work (2011: 11).

Not all coaches use this device (normally a couple of typed pages). Even when plans are constructed, not every organisation asks to see this. Arguing against the development of coaching plans, Brookfield (1986: 213) and Peterson (2002) suggest that personal learning "cannot be specified in advance in terms of objectives to be obtained" as objectives frequently *evolve* during the engagement.

When Coutu & Kauffman (2009) surveyed 140 coaches to understand the realities surrounding executive coaching, they discovered that the focus of coaching typically *shifts* during the course of an engagement and there is a need to continually refine coaching objectives throughout the engagement.

Based on this research, none of the counsellors interviewed use an equivalent format. Other than counsellors who practice CBT, there is seldom any documentation exchanged in therapy. Why?

Three reasons emerged as being particularly important:

o Staying non-directive.

o Avoidance of the term diagnosis.

o Payment practices for work completed.

Staying Non-Directive

The underpinning philosophy across all of the counselling literature states that the therapist should not *impose* a diagnosis or a *solution* on the client. The book *I'm OK, You're OK* captures the essence of this non-directive philosophy (Harris, 1969).

Core Belief

The client has the internal means to solve their own problems. It's too easy for a therapist to become overly solutions-focused and resolve the immediate presenting issue:

> ... all too many of those who seek the help of counsellors have spent much of their lives surrounded by people who, with devastating inappropriateness, have appointed themselves experts in the conduct of other people's lives (Mearns *et al*, 2013: 7).

We have seen earlier that an *interventionist stance* is sometimes supported, even expected, by clients seeking immediate help. Yet, the medium-term goal in both coaching and counselling is creating higher levels of awareness, essentially allowing the client to *self-coach* (Palmer & Szymanska, 2008: 89):

> Because the concept of therapy, and hence of therapists, has been derived from medicine, we have tended to fall into the same error of thinking that the therapist cures the patient. When applied to psychotherapy, or for that matter to psychiatry generally, this is an erroneous notion. In dealing with psychiatric illness there is no treatment that you can apply to a person that will bring about real change in him. The person has to undertake the work himself (Browne, 2008: 261).

It follows that counsellors err on the non-directive *(don't tell)* side of the equation. They essentially dismiss the 'snooker ball' metaphor of clients being bumped around by external forces. The goal is to reinstate *agency*; clients are both capable and responsible for their own actions (Stojnov & Pavlovic, 2010: 137). The family therapist Carl Whitaker famously allowed himself to fall asleep when working, so that the families he worked with would find their own way forward (Hardingham, 1998: 102).

However, this point is not universally accepted. Cavanagh derides overly client-centric approaches that insist the solution is *in the client*, arguing that expert knowledge is critical; without this, the coach is simply a *"well-meaning amateur"* (2005: 337). However, this is a minority opinion.

Based on the literature reviewed, a core philosophical tenet is that both coachees and clients are the "CEOs of their own life" (Mooney, 2008). Yet, there seems to be a *misunderstanding* that writing a coaching plan somehow runs counter to this 'non-directive' stance. My personal experience is that a well-thought-out coaching plan can add real value, with the obvious *caveat* that it needs to be the *coachee's plan*. The potential downside, that the coach might *dominate* the relationship, can happen anyway, irrespective of whether a coaching plan is constructed.

Clear Role

The role of a coach can be confusing to clients – particularly if they have a prior expectation of a Doctor / Patient relationship. It's up to the coach to make it clear that she is not the equivalent of Red Adair – rushing around looking for *fires* (problems) to extinguish. Coaching plans, which can be completed at various levels of abstraction (Locke & Latham, 1990), outline the goals for the intervention and underscore this 'ownership' point. Some people require very *concrete* plans – for example, the need to improve report-writing skills. For others, the aim point may be somewhat *loose* – for example, extracting more meaning from life.

While there is zero contradiction between being non-directive and constructing a coaching plan, this device is *never* applied in counselling other than as a sort of *ground rules* for the therapy:

> ... while one may not have the right or the power to get a person to stop drinking excessively, or to stop them committing suicide, one is perfectly entitled to say, 'If I am to work successfully with you in therapy, I cannot do so if you are drinking heavily, or if you are threatening to commit suicide every time the going gets rough' (Browne, 2008: 273).

Based on this research, none of the therapists produce anything in writing (nor do most of the coaches), other than an initial contract (see **Appendix B**):

When invited by a company to coach an individual I meet with the coachee and the procuring manager. Then I write a proposal. However, this is more for the purpose of agreeing the contract rather than preparing a formal coaching plan" (Coach R).

In line with the 'non-directive' stance, one respondent stated:

I don't do anything formal. If I did have to produce something, I'd ask the coachee to prepare it and present it as his or her own work (Coach N).

A number of people argued against the preparation of coaching plans, citing concerns around *confidentiality*:

I don't believe coaching could be effective if the organisation had to be debriefed from the sessions. That would be a deal-breaker as far as I'm concerned (Coach M).

It raises an obvious question: "If a coaching plan is constructed, who gets to see it?".[9]

Multi-Party Relationship

Those in favour of producing coaching plans argue that it makes the *work* explicit and can provide a *sense of progress* to stakeholders, including the organisation that is funding the initiative.

Coaching is part of the normal business investment landscape. Where leaders are responsible for delivering results, there is an entitlement to know the topics being worked on and, arguably, too much political correctness around protecting the *confessional nature* of the process. A coaching plan allows a three-way (coach; coachee; organisation) or even a four-way (coach; coachee; line manager; HR manager) relationship.

---

[9]   On the general question of taking notes, one coach mentioned a fear of disclosure and potentially getting sued. Some practitioners in the USA avoid note-taking for this reason. Perhaps litigation may become an issue in the future in Ireland, with coaches being called as witnesses in disputed cases. While this is certainly possible, I'm not aware of a single instance of this happening to date.

When plans are explicit, the organisation can support the behavioural changes sought. Essentially, the HR / line managers become *allies* in the change process:

> I meet the coachee for one hour a month, while they spend 40 hours a week in the same office as their boss (Coach J).

Organisations need the line manager to be supportive of the coachee's development long after the coach has departed. Therefore *excluding* the line manager from the process makes little sense. While there is certainly a need to respect confidentiality, this doesn't have to be managed on an all-or-nothing basis. Even where the development plan is shared, discussions that underpin this remain private.

> A final 'organisation level' argument is put forward by Jarvis:
> Unless HR oversees and manages coaching activities it is
> difficult to get a clear picture of what coaching is taking place
> and how effective it is. In such cases, the evaluation of coaching
> activities is impossible and you lose an opportunity to build up a
> body of knowledge about lessons learned (Jarvis *et al*, 2006: 49).

Avoiding *Diagnosis*

There is a general pushback in the counselling literature against the use of the term *diagnosis* and the implicit Doctor / Patient relationship associated with the medical model. Interestingly, many of the pioneers of counselling – for example, Sigmund Freud and Carl Jung – were medical doctors and this terminology was extensively used in their early writings.

In counselling, the *diagnosis* is typically conducted in the mind of the counsellor and may not be directly discussed with the client. Of course, the client can *infer* what the counsellor thinks by the type of questions asked or challenges posed. In contrast, the development of a coaching plan makes the thinking of the coach explicit (the *today* picture and the route to *tomorrow*). By withholding this, therapists in fact may deny clients the full benefit of their insight.

Some coaches, who work to a much shorter timeline, see counselling as a circuitous process. If the client has full access to the therapist face-to-face, why is there a reluctance to allow access to the therapist's thinking in writing? Wouldn't capturing the diagnosis / future goals help to clarify the central issues being addressed? As the work progresses, additional issues or insights may emerge and a coaching plan can be amended to accommodate this.

Overall, my experience suggests that developing a coaching plan is a more democratic approach. It allows the *cards to be played face up* and makes descriptions accessible in layperson terms, avoiding any form of psycho-jargon, which can create a barrier between the therapist and the client (Nelson-Jones, 2000: 11). It also allows the coachee to *challenge* the thinking of the coach. While counselling is supposedly non-directive, sometimes *direction* is simply hidden from the client. It's difficult to challenge something that you can't see and perhaps don't fully understand.

Payment Practices

One final point under this heading may help to explain the reluctance of some professionals to construct coaching plans.

In counselling, clients pay for face-to-face interactions. All of the work happens *in the room* and there is no expectation that additional work will be completed. Anything that takes place outside of this – for example, a therapist sourcing an article on eating disorders for a client – is unpaid. In contrast, in coaching where the organisation picks up the tab, there's generally less sensitivity to how time is allocated. Work completed *outside* of face-to-face coaching is also paid – gathering feedback on the coachee or constructing a coaching plan. The fact that counsellors only get paid for face-to-face time may partly explain the reluctance to construct coaching / therapy plans (albeit this is a *lesser* argument than the non-directiveness / avoiding diagnosis points touched on above).

Case Study F: Ethical Dilemma

I was asked to work with John Jones, a mid-ranking executive in a large commercial organisation. John was neither a star-performer nor an underperformer. In fact, he'd sought coaching for this very reason, feeling his career was *stuck*. As the coaching unfolded, it turned out that he was actually highly ambitious. In fact, his level of ambition seemed to be somewhat higher than his ability.

There is a subtle but important point here. Being 'non-judgemental' means that the coach is not pushing a particular end point – *'you need to have a burning ambition to get to the top of your profession'*. It *doesn't* mean that the coach will not exercise judgement or have an opinion on the coachee's current performance.

When I met with the HR director and John's line manager, they expressed remarkably similar views (I didn't share my thoughts at that point). Quite often, a central part of the coaching role is to instil confidence, to get coachees to question career-limiting assumptions. John's self-esteem was sky-high, at least outwardly, so confidence-building was not the main challenge.

When we gained rapport, he told me that he'd already decided to leave the organisation. Preparations were advanced, including a well-thought-out plan to take a large customer with him, effectively stealing this business from his employer. When John informed me about this, I was immediately conflicted. There were three choices:

o Highlight the ethical dilemma for John – albeit my initial efforts to argue this seemed to have very little traction.

o Get him to consider the potential downsides – for example, future legal claims from the employer and reputational damage to himself.

o Whistleblow – inform the organisation about John's plan; then walk away and allow them resolve this issue internally.

For just over a week, I wrestled with this dilemma, confused about how best to respond. The organisation was a good client. I'd already coached a number of executives and hoped to work there in the future. While I didn't particularly warm to him, neither my personal relationship with John nor a wish to secure future business from the organisation offered a solid rationale for breaking a confidence. Then, somewhat out of the blue, John secured a role in a completely different industry. He left the company abruptly, at short notice. The problem had resolved itself and I was off the hook!

QUESTION #4: ARE THE CORE PROCESSES DIFFERENT?

What happens when a new coachee or client enters the office? Do coaches and counsellors start from the same place? Is *'the way the work gets done'* radically different across the coaching / counselling divide? While there is no absolute answer to this question, the following broad approaches are used by both coaches (therapeutic model) and counsellors.

Unconditional Positive Regard

The term *unconditional positive regard,* coined by Carl Rogers *circa* 1957, has become the mantra in both coaching and counselling. Wilkins argues that this concept is not new *per se*, suggesting that it's closely associated with forgiveness and compassion, core tenets of many established religions (2000: 25). It provides a foundation of respect, the overall orientation of coaches / counsellors towards clients that should remain in place while they work together.

Mearns & Thorne offer a very clear definition of what it means:

> Unconditional positive regard is the label given to the fundamental attitude of the person-centred counsellor towards her client. The counsellor who holds this attitude deeply values the humanity of her client and is not deflected in that valuing by any particular client behaviours. The attitude manifests itself in the counsellor's consistent acceptance of and enduring warmth towards her client (1988: 59).

Mearns later made a useful distinction between *accepting* someone and *liking* them. Liking is normally based on shared values or complimentary needs; the role for counsellors is to be *beside* their client, not necessarily *on their side* (1994: 54).

This philosophy can be differentiated from *conditional regard*: '*I will like you when you begin to do what I suggest*'. The education sector provides an example of this idea in practice. For many teachers, it's easy to like bright, well-behaved students. They do what they're told, produce assignments on time and the quality of output is seen to reflect well on the professional. The central question is *Can you love* all *of your students?* A similar challenge is posed for coaches and counsellors:

> A distressed, bored or unengaged therapist is in danger of
> offering unconditional positive disregard (Wilkins, 2000: 26).

The psychoanalytical concept here is the *dead mother*, where a child born following the death of a sibling is not *seen*. Schutzenberger argues that very often the child of this *dead mother* will have a difficult life, suicidal tendencies or suffer from schizophrenia (1991: 208). While less extreme, the withholding of unconditional positive regard may make a client feel that they don't have a *right* to therapy or that the coach or counsellor doesn't want to work with them and is simply going through the motions.

Wilkins, in helping to further refine this concept, argues: "... being person-centred is not about being passive or 'nice'" (*op cit*: 31) and it certainly doesn't preclude *challenge*. Implicit in this is the acceptance of the other person's right *not to* change.

It follows that unconditional positive regard, while outwardly simple, actually poses an incredibly high standard. It's relatively easy when we encounter *good* coachees or clients, but much more difficult with some people who present for support:

> The reason that psychotherapeutic interventions are seen not to
> 'work' with, for example, people in psychotic state and
> paedophiles, may have much more to do with the belief, fear,
> disapproval and revulsion of the therapists than with the
> supposed intractable nature of the clients. However open-minded
> therapists believe themselves to be, however tolerant they are, if
> the client does not experience unconditional positive regard, then
> the likelihood is that the therapy will fail (*op cit*, 32).

In similar vein, Shainberg argues:

Supervisees come to see that it is their own thoughts that are at times their greatest enemies in the treatment process (1985: 175).

In the words of Pogo, the USA-based comic-strip character:

We have met the enemy and he is us (Kelly, 1971).

No Difference

Unconditional positive regard is a foundation stone for good coaching and counselling. During the data collection phase, there was no difference between the coaching / counselling professionals on this point. I asked both groups whether they had ever *refused* to work with a client because of their 'presenting issues'.

The responses focused on *areas of specialism,* rather than *disgust.* For example, Therapist T said that she doesn't work with clients dealing with a drug addiction or 'active alcoholics', believing that these conditions need specialist input that she couldn't provide.

Life History

In commencing a new relationship, one general approach to data gathering can be labelled as *life history.* To get a better understanding of the presenting issues, the coachee / client is asked to relate their story. In the counselling arena this can sometimes be quite detailed, including the construction of genograms, a family-tree graphic that illustrates the mental health history of the client's family going back several generations (McGoldrick *et al,* 2008).

This approach offers several benefits. It allows the client to *tell their story,* becoming involved in the sessions straight away. People who attend coaching / counselling for the first time are often nervous and this quickly eases them into the process. Second, it's relatively easy for the professional involved to grasp the overall picture; we recall *stories* better than seemingly unrelated facts. Third, it allows the coach or therapist to identify *themes.* Gathering data in this *timeline* approach allows repetitions to emerge.

Cavanagh argues: "Coaching is a journey in search of patterns" (2005: 313). The central idea in psychotherapy is that *inner tapes* play on a continual loop, often reflecting the *learned roles* a person played in an earlier part of their life (*nurturer, rescuer, the wild one* and so on). The Barnardo's tagline – 'Every childhood lasts a lifetime' –,communicates this. Once these unconscious patterns become visible, the coachee / client can *decide* whether particular behaviours are relevant in their current life.

A central idea in counselling is that no child gets all its needs met; there is always some *psychological deficit*. In the best-case scenario, the *deficits* are relatively minor and we overcome or learn to live with these. In cases of severe deprivation – for example, where children are born into dysfunctional families – this early experience can negatively impact an entire life. To survive in family or institutional environments, children make *creative adjustments* (the descriptive term used by Gestalt counsellors) that make sense *at that time*. So, we learn to think and behave in a particular way early on. Without being consciously aware of this, some people continue to *travel* the same route all their lives. Because of the *familiarity* and *comfort* offered, the pattern is often repeated over and over, even where the person outwardly rails against this:

> It is what Freud called the 'repetition compulsion', the magnetic summons of an old wound in our lives that has so much energy, such a familiar script, and such a predictable outcome attached to it that we feel obliged to relive it or pass it on to our children (Hollis, 2005: 81).

Simon & Garfunkel, making essentially the same point, sang in *Keep The Customer Satisfied*, "It's the same old story, everywhere I go" (1971). For example, a person who makes the statement "I don't do feelings" might have developed an outwardly *cold* persona as a way to reduce the hurt of not feeling loved. While they may acknowledge (intellectually) that poor connection skills can limit careers, they often feel *powerless* to change. In similar vein, someone who is overly self-critical (*"I'm useless at everything"*) may accept these negative messages as if they were *truth*, despite reams of counter-evidence – for example, university or technical qualifications.

A centrally-important point is that thinking and behavioural patterns that *currently* exist can often be understood against a *historical* backdrop. To break negative patterns, we first need to unearth these *mental tapes* and critically examine what was *recorded* during an earlier period. Counsellors trained in the psychotherapeutic tradition are likely to default to this *life history* approach. Coaches may or may not use this approach (the shorter timeframe in coaching doesn't always allow it). Regardless of the approach taken, the professionals are trying to get a deep understanding of the coachee / client in order to support their forward journey. On the assumption that a negative pattern of behaviour can be uncovered, the role for the coach or therapist is often to explain three related ideas to a coachee or client:

o   This defence was once very important.

o   But it's now hurting you.

o   It may no longer be necessary (Cozolino, 2004:145).

Case Study G: New Manager

Emmet Emerson was struggling in his new job. While he'd previously led a number of project teams, this was his first real foray into line management. He was unfamiliar with the core task (software development) in a new department and the group *inherited* seemed unmotivated. In his own words, he was "failing miserably". Overall, Emmet seemed diligent. He was precise in his dress code and asked detailed questions during the contracting phase (how diary dates were booked, how the billing worked and so on). He smiled a lot and initially seemed more concerned about me than about himself. It provided an early clue about his style.

What subsequently emerged were two central ideas implanted in Emmet's *mental tapes*:

o   You can't manage someone unless you understand *everything* they do.

o   *Positive people perform better* and it's the manager's job to keep everyone happy.

His father had been a stickler for detail. Emmet interpreted this as a need to *fully understand everything that people do*; this was the *only* way to manage people. The second issue took a little more time to unearth. It turned out that Emmet had essentially played the *good son* role in his original family. He wanted to *please* his parents to avoid their constant bickering, which, as a child, he found stressful. Many years later, differences of opinion among staff made him very anxious and he did everything in his power to *stop* this, even when internal debates and conflict around core business ideas were legitimate and useful.

Emmet was essentially crushing himself under the weight of two mistaken beliefs:

- o He needed to *fully* understand complex technology that was not part of his baseline training.

- o He needed to *please* a group of people who viewed his efforts to motivate them as a sign of managerial weakness.

Once these ideas were surfaced, Emmet came to a very different understanding of how this group should be led and became successful in the role.

Anxiety: Hot Buttons

Another approach, rooted in the *here and now* (what's happening in *this* room for both parties), is labelled Gestalt therapy, the school of counselling most commonly associated with Fritz Perls (Perls *et al*, 1994). Under this heading, the opening salvo might be along the lines of "What brought you here today?".

The rationale for following a *right now* approach is that clients are driven to seek therapy for a reason. Understanding that reason, the *anxiety hot spot*, is the most powerful place to begin. By 'keeping it real', coaches and therapists guard against working on some abstract ideal that, because of its attractiveness, can seem to justify ignoring where the person is right now, what Krishnamurti labels "an accepted and respectable postponement" (1991: 60). Imagine approaching someone who'd just been involved in a traffic accident and commenting "You should consider eating more bran; it's so good for digestion". The 'right now' approach focuses on the accident rather than the cereal.

Invisible Patterns

Working on the 'hot button' shares a fundamental idea with the timeline approach sketched earlier – thinking and behavioural patterns follow a path that's often invisible to the coachee / client. They essentially *'repeat their normal behavioural patterns'* in the here-and-now relationship with the therapist and, in this way, the path forward (and the past) is revealed.

Collecting historical data, as per the life history approach, is unnecessary, almost a waste of time when a *richer* source of first-hand data exists within the room. This becomes understood through questions like *What's happening for you right now?* and *If you stay with that for a bit longer, what else can you see?*. The power of this approach is evoked in Yalom's description that the *here and now* feelings are to the experienced therapist "... of as much use as a microscope is to the microbiologist" (1975: 149).

Of course, sometimes a new coachee or client simply wants to get something *off their chest* and there may be an enforced period of *listening* before any decision on *approach* is made. An attempt to *steer* the conversation can feel like an interruption, with the coach / therapist communicating *"Let's move on from what you are saying and get to the important stuff"* (whatever the client is saying at any moment in time is the important stuff).

Both the *timeline* and the *anxiety* approaches, while outwardly different, share a common heritage. While the psychodynamic tradition pays more attention to history and the Gestalt school puts more focus on *what's happening right now*, both approaches work on the premise that underlying thinking patterns drive behaviour.

Use of Self

Interestingly, this 'here and now' concept can also be applied by the professional. Across the coaching / counselling divide, meetings with clients can be understood on two levels. **Level 1** focuses on the *story* - how is the coachee / client describing their problem / circumstance? **Level 2** asks *What am I* experiencing *right now?* (labelled *'the use of self')*. The coach / counsellor is asking "Am I bored, excited, sad?" and so on. In relation to this second level, Bluckert argues:

I regard the use of self as the highest order coaching skill. It can be the difference between good and great coaching (2006: 84).

The 'anxiety hot button' approach (working in the 'here and now') is equally available to both coaches and counsellors.

Relationship Depth

There is a strong crossover between coaching and counselling in terms of the depth of the relationship established. Both coaches and counsellors pay enormous attention to what's happening in *this* relationship. Even where the topic is relatively straightforward, the *quality* of the relationship between the coach and the coachee is *differentiated* from normal interpersonal interactions. There are not many settings where someone can experience *unconditional positive regard*, where their needs and aspirations are *fully understood* and where the professional is seeking to work with the coachee / client *without judgement*.

In this area of listening and understanding, coaches have much to learn from therapy:

When functioning best, the therapist is so much inside the private world of the other that he or she can clarify not only the meanings of which the client is aware but even those just below the level of awareness (Kirschenbaum & Land-Henderson, 1990: 136).

The intent here is not solely empathy, but diagnosis. Understanding what's happening in *this* relationship helps the coach or counsellor to speculate about the quality of relationships this person has with others – for example, the immediate relationship is seen as a microcosm of the person's life. When working at their best, coaches / counsellors are not simply responding to the immediate request for support but are using this as part of a broader data collection canvas. The skill here is to *accept* the presenting issues at face value while, at the same time, remaining *detached* and *objective* around how best to support the person going forward. Under this relationship heading, there is very little difference between coaches and counsellors (albeit the counselling relationship is *typically* longer with many more contact points).

Role Modelling

So, how does this 'high-quality relationship' actually work in terms of helping the coachee or client to resolve issues? Assuming a successful 'connection' is made, the counsellor and the client learn how to relate, authentically, warmly, non-judgmentally. The shift or breakthrough for the client comes when they recognise the *potential* – what can be achieved in a healthy relationship. The client, having experienced a successful relationship (which the therapist has essentially *role modelled*), is able to reproduce this in other key relationships that they *repair* or *build* from scratch.

Several assumptions here are worth exploring:

o First, the relationship with the coach or counsellor needs to *work*.

o Second, the coachee / client needs to understand *why* this is working.

o Finally, the coachee / client needs to be able to *replicate this* with key people in their outside life, people who may never have experienced 'high-level' functioning (unconditional positive regard and so on).

For me, the idea that the coachee or client can simply *transplant* this new 'high-quality' relationship idea into other parts of their life is optimistic, perhaps even somewhat naïve. It's hugely dependant on the 'social capital' (support) that they have externally. Personally, I struggle with the idea that simply creating *awareness* as a stand-alone intervention can bring about change and I lean closer to the argument that insight is necessary, but not sufficient (Kahn, 1997: 4). In my experience, coachees often require more intervention – formal coaching plans or CBT templates to make change happen (Kegan & Lahey, 2009).

Hurdle Questions

Where a coachee is struggling with an issue, experiencing difficulty in thinking it through or having limited experience to draw on, I believe it's legitimate to add *suggestions* into the mix. However, to ensure that this stops short of 'telling' becoming the default mode, some *stress test* questions can be useful, what one respondent described as *"relying on your inner supervisor"* (Therapist Q). For example:

o **Q: Fully Understand:** Have we spent sufficient time *bottoming out* the issue? Are we rushing to a solution? Why am I feeling pressure to progress this right now?

o **Q: Self-Sufficiency:** Do I feel that the client will not be able to solve this issue on their own? Based on what evidence?

o **Q: Why Intervene?:** Is there something going on inside *me* that is driving this - trying to look *smart* or this topic is making me *uncomfortable*?

Self-Sufficiency

To repeat, a core assumption in counselling (and therapeutic coaching) is that the client is self-sufficient. Under conditions of acceptance and support, each person is seen to have an innate capacity to evolve in a *healthful* direction. Using their own positive energy and insight, people discover the best solution for themselves (Milner *et al*, 2013).

While there is zero argument in favour of a process where the counsellor or coach *dominates* the client, is the assumption that coachees / clients *always* have the correct answer within them fully justified? In trying to trace the root of this, the concept seems to have been influenced by the Socratic method of teaching. This ancient form of discourse (the method is over 2,400 years old) was based on Socrates' belief that lecturing was not an effective method of teaching *all* students. Socrates valued the knowledge and understanding already present. Helping students examine their biases and beliefs improved reasoning skills and promoted more rational thinking (Copeland, 2005: 7). Somewhere along the line, this *teaching pedagogy* (which applied to *some* students) has morphed into a mantra of *"Don't ever give advice to any client"*. Is this always the correct stance?

Consider the following example: Stacey Radin is a prominent New York City-based executive coach. She draws on her research and work with 150+ women leaders across the USA who have succeeded in scaling various corporate ladders. In working with female clients, should this historical data *disappear* because the clients are assumed to already know the answers? Presumably, the reason that some clients are attracted to work with Dr. Radin in the first place is to seek this exact information (Keddy & Johnson, 2011: 98).

My strong sense is that external knowledge and wisdom can be useful additional inputs that the coach / counsellor adds into the mix. The *trick* is knowing when to intervene and when to do nothing, straddling the grey line that sits between asking questions and supplying answers. Determining the correct response is more art than science, part of the intrigue of working in this space.

Practice Difference: Looking Forward

A critique of the therapeutic approaches sketched above is that they over-focus on *problems* in people's lives and miss the value of focusing on *strengths* (Lee, 2009). In contrast, positive psychology offers a different route, what been described as:

> Shifting attention away from pathology and pain and directing
> it toward a clear-eyed concentration on strength, vision, and
> dreams ... what energises and pulls people forward (Kauffman,
> 2006: 220).

Coaching, typically more *future-focused,* is arguably a better fit with this idea. Yet the obvious *caveat* in ignoring the past is that hidden patterns can re-emerge and unravel progress made. While there are a range of views around the usefulness of 'mining the past', the argument that counselling is *yesterday-* / *today*-focused while coaching is today- / *tomorrow*-focused is broadly correct and differentiates the two disciplines.

Segmentation Approach

Regardless of the starting point (life history *versus* anxiety hot buttons), it's sometimes useful to *segment* the presenting issues. For a coachee presenting with several issues, the realisation that a *finite* number of issues are causing concern may provide psychological comfort. Wrestling with three difficult issues is easier to cope with than thinking "My entire life is in chaos". Segmentation brings clarity around individual issues, helping to ease the burden. Further, ranking issues in priority order – making a determination about what would make the *most* difference to the coachee / client if it was *fixed* – focuses attention on areas with the highest change potential. To overstate, if a house was on fire while the owner simultaneously had been thinking about upgrading the living room, it's important to know where to pay attention.

There are two potential downsides to a segmentation approach. First, the sessions can become overly intellectual. When a coachee / client attends, often in an anxious or troubled state, the last thing they need is to encounter someone who is all *head* and no *heart*, parsing their worries into neat little boxes without identifying with their feelings; empathy cannot be by-passed. Segmentation risks turning the client into an '*it*' and can lead to what Pelham describes as "... the danger of rehearsing the next question instead of really listening to what is being said now" (2014: 33). Working in an intellectual way can make the coachee / client feel like an object being worked *on* rather than a person being worked *with*. Shainberg outlines a conversation with a trainee therapist who described this mechanistic style: "So, I felt the patient way, way out there, like a piece of equipment to be fixed and I had to find the right parts" (1985: 173). Second, while both coaches and counsellors help to navigate the *problem*, a key philosophical point is that the *button for change* is on the inside. The coachee or client decides *what is and what isn't* important and whether or not to change their pattern (Mooney, 2008: 76): "The role of the counsellor is to support the journey that the client wants to make" (Therapist Y). However, with these *caveats* noted, segmentation can be useful in helping some coachees / clients unpack issues into easily digestible chunks.

Practice Difference: Data Collection

Very significant differences emerged between coaching and counselling around 'data collection'. Coaches use a variety of *approaches* and *tools* that often involve other people (for example, 360^0 feedback).

In counselling, data collection is completed one-on-one with the therapist taking a personal history or working in the 'here and now' to uncover data with the client. The subjective world of the client is deemed to be more important than understanding how anyone else feels about the client's performance.

In coaching, a wide variety of psychometric instruments/tools are available: EQ-I, Myers-Briggs (MBTI), Talent Q, Dimensions Personality Tests, MVS Self-Assessment Tool, Strengthscope, DISC, Enneagram and the HAY Model were all mentioned by respondents. Some coaches, including myself, prefer to use a customised 360^0 approach designed for the individual client, with data being collected in direct interviews rather than on-line.

Why do coaches use psychometric instruments? The central purpose is to gather data to present to the client: "They provide a platform for a discussion which can otherwise feel unsafe" (Coach H). This idea of safety / security for the coach was picked up by a couple of respondents. One coach suggested that:

> The size of the interest in psychometric tools is directly
> proportional to the level of anxiety in the coach. Inexperienced
> coaches cling to these like a life raft in the Atlantic (Coach J).

Typically, coaches 'in favour' of psychometrics were *users* while those who were less enamoured didn't use any instrumentation (in itself, hardly a surprising finding).

Getting Physical

While it's impossible to be precise in terms of actual numbers, psychoanalysis (an elongated form of therapy) now represents a very small percentage of the counselling market.

In the early days of psychoanalysis, the therapist sat directly behind the client who lay on a couch, eyes closed, free from external distractions. Minimum disruption to the free association of thoughts supposedly allowed an insight into the client's *unconscious*. Some early years practitioners also slept with their patients as part of the therapy. Quite apart from ethical considerations around exploiting vulnerability, the consensus now is that this level of *closeness* is fraught with difficulty and is universally frowned upon. While some therapists maintain a complete ban on physical contact (for example, a no-handshake rule), most argue this *distant* style of therapy violates the goal of building a normal relationship. While less extreme, many counsellors keep the consulting room free of family pictures or other personal memorabilia in order to present a *blank canvas* to the client. Both coaches and counsellors generally sit facing clients in a comfortable setting, much like you would share a coffee with a friend.

Yet, physicality has an additional dimension – as a way to collect data. For example, physical therapy (art, body movement, the use of props like the empty chair technique in Gestalt) requires clients becoming *active*. The central purpose is to *access inner thoughts or conflicts,* insights that don't always emerge in conventional settings. For example, during one exercise completed at University College Dublin, we were asked to draw a picture that explained our life journey. Using the metaphor of a river, I captured the significant events in my life, commencing at the source (birth) and as the river flowed towards the sea (death). What was striking about this exercise was the way in which emotionally-charged events and key questions were quickly highlighted.

Non-verbal approaches allow us to see connections, unlocking our inner world, sometimes in a way that was closed off to us in the past. The rationale is simple. You can't fix a problem you don't understand. We are not simply a brain; body language can provide useful additional insight to the therapist and client. Freud noted:

> He that has eyes to see and ears to hear may convince himself
> that no mortal may keep a secret. If his lips are silent, he
> chatters with his fingertips (1905: 77).

In another training exercise, we used toy figures (soldiers, farm animals, dolls) to *replicate* the family we grew up in. The figures chosen by each person captured key family dynamics (dominant father; a loving mother conflicted between nurturing needs *versus* the wish to be professionally successful; being the favourite child and so on).

Moving from an *intellectual* towards an *emotional understanding* can provide the spark that lights the fire of change:

> The gut level of vital energy is required to help us go beyond feeling that something is important, to feeling it is absolutely necessary to address the adaptive changes revealed (Reams, 2009: 174).

Practice Difference: Body Movement

Under this heading we find a substantial difference between coaching and counselling. Only two of the coaches met during this research used any type of non-verbal approaches. Why?

The shorter timelines involved don't explain this as there is no indication these techniques are slower (it's actually the reverse). The critical issue that emerged during the research was essentially a *fear of looking foolish*. Many coaches simply don't have the baseline training in these techniques to demonstrate mastery. Because of this, they avoid using approaches where they feel unsure, fearful that they would communicate discomfort or, even worse, *amateurishness*.

This issue provides a perfect example of the need for a deeper level of training for coaches, helping them understand and incorporate techniques that originated in counselling which can be usefully deployed in coaching.

QUESTION #5: IS THE ENGAGEMENT STYLE DIFFERENT?

The research indicates a grain of truth in the stereotype that coaches *tell* while counsellors primarily *listen*.

This applies, in particular, to coaches who follow the instructional model (where there's no perceived contradiction in *telling* coachees what to do). Under this heading, coaches contribute directly to brainstorming, adding experience gained in working with other clients or from their own careers.

In contrast, those who operate the therapeutic coaching model are in *active listening* mode every bit as much as counsellors. We don't complete homework for our kids; they learn to do it themselves. In similar vein, adults learn (primarily) by *doing*. This highly reflective way of coaching is suitable for competent, self-aware coaches who operate the therapeutic model.

However, *all* coaches, regardless of orientation, are under more time pressure as the process is *telescoped vis-à-vis* counselling. Where coaches become overly conscious of the organisation as the client, they may strive to deliver value for money, *demonstrating* expertise in a short / sharp timeframe. It's also possible that coaches unconsciously close down areas of enquiry due to personal discomfort with the issues under discussion – 'moving on' can be a form of *avoidance*.

While the exact same challenges apply to therapists, the fact that they have spent longer *working on themselves* (and in understanding the power of counter-transference) equips them better to avoid these particular tripwires. Arguably, following a process of elongated training, therapists become more comfortable dealing with their own and their client's *discomfort*.

Coaches Challenge More?

While both coaches and counsellors *listen*, do coaches *challenge* more? Core argument = *challenge* provides the *raison d'être* of coaching. The title of Marshall Goldsmith's book *What Got You Here Won't Get You There* (2008) captures the essence of the coaching task.

Central Idea

Coachees *need to change and* coaches *challenge them* to make this happen. If I never allow my kids to go into the city, I am assured they will always be safe. Yet, by taking this stance, I deny them the opportunity to become independent learners. The corollary in coaching is that awareness and learning is often most potent when issues raised are *close to the edge of the cliff,* beyond the psychological comfort that comes from staying in a known behavioural *pattern*. By staying *too safe* (a metaphorical *mile* from the cliff edge), opportunities for new insights are lost. The *primary* task is to help people overcome maladaptive and distorted perceptions. Rather than adopting an overly *supportive* role, coaches and therapists should confront any circularity in client's thinking (Auerbach, 2006). If active listening and unconditional positive regard were all that was required for change to happen, the psychology around transference, unconscious process and so on essentially would be redundant. These *concepts* are brought into play when coachees / clients are *challenged to change*. In a sense, the challenge allows both coaches and counsellors to 'test' whether the material they are working on is hitting the spot.

The early part of the work is a time of *active listening*. This has a dual benefit. Firstly, it's diagnostic, helping the coach / counsellor to understand the presenting issues. It's also empathic, communicating interest, reinforcing a sense of worth. Across the coaching / counselling divide, no-holds-barred conversations make issues *discussible*. Under this heading, the coach / therapist may form a hunch (hypothesis) about the central presenting issues, or ideas that may be helpful in terms of moving forward. It could involve a pattern of behaviour unconsciously repeated from an earlier period. It might be a need to reframe a problem – for example, taking personal ownership rather than outsourcing *blame*. Sometimes it's encouragement to face up to a difficult life decision. As the sessions unfold and the relationship deepens, powerful conversations go beyond listening. There's often a subtle shift, a *challenge* to how the coachee / client sees the world, which can become uncomfortable. Gendlin captures this when he argues:

> It isn't enough that the patient repeats with the therapist his maladjusted feelings and ways of setting up interpersonal situations. After all, the patient is said to repeat these with everyone in his life, and not only with the therapist. Thus, the sheer repeating, even when it is a concrete reliving, doesn't yet resolve anything. Somehow, with the therapist, the patient doesn't only repeat; he gets beyond the repeating. He doesn't only relive; he lives further, if he resolves problems experientially (1968: 222).

Mackewn, agreeing that the therapist's role needs to be interventionist, makes a similar point:

> Many clients come for counselling or therapy wanting to blame others for their predicament, feeling like victims of societal pressures or poor parenting and hoping to get their needs met by someone else – often the counsellor or therapist. They are genuinely ignorant about the whole concept of self responsibility and may have little or no idea that they play an active role in organising their psychological reality (Mackewn, 1997: 124-125).

Leadership Role

In relation to *challenging* clients, executive coaches have a duty to move issues towards resolution. Coaching is not a fireside chat; it invites individuals to stretch out of their comfort zone. Too much focus on *safety* conflicts with the requirement to help coachees address what may be very difficult issues. Spinelli & Horner suggest that:

> ... it is wise for coaches to bear in mind that, sometimes, the change solutions that are offered can create far greater distress and unease in living than did the presenting issue (2008: 121-122).

Sandler, taking up this point, argues that to be fully effective, coaching needs to go beyond the creation of positive regard; the ability to identify closely with the client should be balanced with retaining responsibility for addressing the client's work-related goals and tasks (2011: 52). At its core, coaching represents the creation of a powerful *working alliance* (Horvat *et al*, 1994). In challenging the coachee to maximise potential, the coaching role is therefore one of *leadership* as well as *partnership* (Sandler, 2011: 64).

It follows that coaching or counselling should not simply be measured by whether the client is happy or not. Good *consulting* (which is enormously *directive*) can produce happy clients. The key measure of success is whether the coach / counsellor has empowered a client to resolve future issues using their own resources. Being *real* with the coachee / client – including challenging their thinking at appropriate junctures – is the ultimate test of whether the coach is fully present.

Arguably, the most potentially damaging feature of coaching or counselling is insincerity, involving what Eric Berne described as "marshmallow-throwing" and other writers have labelled "plastic strokes" (Stewart & Jones, 2012: 80). The core skill is challenging in a way that's helpful rather than destructive:

> Metaphorically, the person-centered counsellor wants to 'knock on the client's door' at a deeper level of his experiencing but she does not want to knock the door down (Mearns *et al*, 2013: 60).

Case Study H: Looking Inwards

Tim Twomey sought support to help him deal with *bullying*. His manager, a tough taskmaster, was certainly at the upper end of demanding. Tim spent considerable time and seemed comfortable telling me about this "brutal boss", recounting numerous examples of inconsiderate, last-minute requests, stating why his boss wasn't a 'nice person' (the language used was slightly more colourful). In a sense, Tim was inviting me into a game called *Isn't my boss terrible?*. Each time we met, I was expected to play the same role (sympathiser). After I'd heard the baseline story and empathised, an idea started to emerge. Tim was assigning negative feelings to his boss that he actually felt about himself, insecurities about his own ability to perform this mid-level (but complex) role. A range of feelings were *attributed* (technically *projected into*) the boss, even though Tim's boss had never actually said any of this. When we moved onto the topic of Tim himself rather than the bad behaviour of the boss, we began to tap into a much richer seam of material. Eventually, after more than 14 sessions, Tim was able to understand and deal with his own insecurities and build a much more positive (fact-based) relationship with his boss. It's all too easy to export blame. Neither coaching nor counselling should be a sanctuary for delusion.

A working hypothesis allows the coach / therapist to *test* whether the behaviour of the person they are working with can be explained. All behaviour has a payoff; understanding this – bringing it *into view* – allows the coachee or client at least to consider something that might have been hidden. In the language of Gestalt, it allows the *ground* (background) to become *figure* (foreground).[10] Working in this way allows the coach / therapist to challenge the thinking or behaviour of the client in a way that's perceived as helpful, despite the fact that the terms *support* and *challenge* seem outwardly contradictory. Of course, timing needs to be added into the mix:

> Even if you pick up a clue, there is a question of timing around
> exactly when you introduce this. 'Right' may not mean right
> now (Pelham, 2014).

The timing issue was particularly important with Tim Twomey. While he eventually came to see that he was the central character in the storyline (rather than his boss), offering this 'analysis' early on would probably have derailed the assignment. Perls *et al* (1994) make the point that the aim of counselling is not to *cure* the client but to teach them how to learn about themselves and to equip them with tools, so that they can solve both present and future problems. Interestingly, Perls often spelt the word responsibility as *response-ability* to underscore this point (Mackewn, 1997: 124).

---

[10] Jenny Stacey, psychotherapist and trainer, UCD, in conversation with the author, April 2014.

Training & Timing

While the importance of challenge is noted, does the evidence from the field research suggest that coaches challenge *more* than therapists? If clients also need to wrestle with issues brought into therapy, why would there be *less challenge* in that forum?

The twin arguments here are training and timing. In relation to training, counsellors undergo professional training over three or four years at undergraduate level. During this time, the concepts of unconditional positive regard and being non-directive essentially become *tattooed* into the thinking of the therapist (regardless of the *school* of counselling studied). Coaches, on the other hand, typically come from the ranks of management consultants or business where challenge is more normal:

> In environments where the onus is on 'getting the job done', it's perhaps understandable that cutting to the chase with bold instruction is the management style of choice for many (Keddy & Johnson, 2011: 13).

With no mandatory training for the role, and arguably less compunction around this, coaches are *more likely* to challenge.

Second, the very different *timeframes* at play may be a factor in the *high-challenge* accusation levelled at coaches. Shorter coaching interventions offer less face-to-face time compared to the more elongated process of counselling. The additional time available in counselling allows clients to come to their own view around what needs to be done. It's not that therapists *don't challenge* clients; rather, in coaching the challenges come sooner, driven by tighter timeframes.

While it's difficult to be definitive, on the basis of the evidence collected, the assertion that coaches *challenge* more is certainly plausible.

QUESTION #6: HOW DO ORGANISATIONS CHOOSE THE PERFECT COACH OR COUNSELLOR?

To answer the question '*How do I choose the best coach for the job?*', buyers navigate unregulated territory. The wide variety of professional qualifications and the fact that the process cannot be witnessed directly are barriers to effective decision-making. It's certainly easier to select counsellors based on formal qualifications. Given these constraints, the phrase *caveat emptor* applies in spades.

Feedback from *buyers* in this research suggests the following selection criteria:

o   Track record.

o   Competence and credibility.

o   Structured approach.

o   What works?

o   Chemistry meetings.

o   Ongoing training.

o   Ongoing supervision.

o   Interpersonal style.

o   Evaluation processes.

o   Return on investment.

Track Record

The first question is often *Has this person delivered in the past?*. Establishing the coach's / counsellor's track record – for example, by reference checking – falls into the *boring, but effective* category. Has this person worked for you before and produced good results? Who else have they worked with? What type of projects did they complete and what results were produced? While it's difficult to make a 'scientific' judgement (the paucity of formal evaluation was highlighted earlier), working with someone you have worked with before and who *understands the organisation culture*, are both strong selling points.

Competence & Credibility

If the coach or counsellor is unknown, competence and credibility seem to be central selection criteria. Under the competence heading, purchasers were primarily focused on business experience, what one respondent labelled as *"contextual expertise"* (Purchaser A). Formal qualifications were also in the mix: "If the coach doesn't invest in himself, why would we take him seriously?" (Purchaser D).

When asked whether someone with a pure psychology background would likely add more value, the general response was that this might be a better fit with counselling.

Under the credibility heading, coming from a similar background (organisation level) and having coaching experience in the specific industry were both mentioned as being 'helpful'.

Structured Approach

Some sophisticated purchasers ask coaches / counsellors to describe their *method* as a way to gain insight into the provider's underpinning philosophy. Changes to the method incorporated over time may indicate a *"reflective practitioner"* (Purchaser B).

While some coaches / counsellors follow a particular model, others have developed a *hybrid style*, the option chosen being dictated by client needs. One therapist argued that he was a *'whiteboard'* – he didn't impose his style on the client (Therapist X). However, the fact that most have studied a particular *school* and overlaid this with their own personality makes the whiteboard analogy *aspirational* for most practitioners:

The tragedy of psychiatry and psychotherapy in its present stage
of development is that the form of therapy offered to the patient
is more likely to be that which the therapist espouses and is
trained in than that which the patient actually needs (Browne,
2008: 319).

Smith (1993) also called attention to the importance of individual
training, suggesting that the 'decision' around how to address client
needs (for example, Cognitive Behavioural Therapy *versus* a
psychoanalytic approach) is more often driven by the counsellor
rather than the client.

In this research, none of the purchasers focused on these *fine-
grained* selection criteria. Was this because most purchasers are not
trained coaches or counsellors? Perhaps it partly explains this finding.
More importantly, several respondents made the point that particular
skills – for example, the ability to be confrontational *and* supportive,
ethics around maintaining confidentiality (and so on) – are *person-
centered*, rather than an outcome of particular 'technical' training.

What Works?

In counselling there have been numerous research efforts to
determine the relative *efficacy* of various approaches. The evidence
that exists points to a surprising conclusion; empathy, rather than
adherence to any particular *school*, represents the 'X Factor' in client
progress, neatly summarised as "We need to walk alongside them,
before they can hear us" (Hardingham, 1998: 15). Coaches and
therapists of all persuasions should take comfort from this. It may
help to overcome what Shainberg describes as "... the common fear
that one is not doing therapy the right way" (1985: 164).

Clients who feel listened to and understood, who experience
unconditional positive regard, make most progress. This
fundamental orientation, rather than adherence to any particular
school, is the best predictor of a successful outcome. Half a century
ago, Carl Rogers echoed this:

Perhaps the deepest of these learnings is a confirmation ... that
therapy has to do with the relationship, and has relatively little to
do with techniques or with theory and ideology (1967: 185-186).

This is sometimes expressed as 'Clients don't care how much you know, until they know how much you care'.

Purchasers of services get an insight into the orientation of the coach or counsellor by asking reflective questions about their own contact:

o How was I treated?

o Was the coach / counsellor able to establish full contact - being present in the here-and-now of our conversation?

o How would I rate the listening skills demonstrated?

o Did they understand *my* needs?

o Did the person seem distracted or overtly trying to sell?

In buying a process that is largely 'invisible', it is not surprising that the purchasers place significant weight on what they can objectively measure – their own relationship with the person offering the service.

Chemistry Meetings

Practices differed around the question of whether coachees were directly involved in the selection of the coach. One organisation asks coachees to review three coach profiles. They then meet two people and make the final selection. Another organisation chooses the coach and gives the coachee the 'right of veto':

We don't put staff in a sweet shop. And we can't abuse coaches by taking up huge chunks of unpaid time (Purchaser D).

In general, there was a recognition that the 'chemistry' between the coach and the coachee was an important part of the mix, and this works both ways:

I've refused to work with a client if, after the chemistry meeting, I find that I cannot easily relate to them. I suggest they consider finding someone else. It's a two-way street (Coach O).

While I understand this viewpoint, personally I've never taken this stance. I'm normally intrigued by what was *blocking* the initial relationship and whether this was a counter-transference issue (something in me rather than in the client). Chemistry meetings are also a feature in counselling – but the client pays for the initial session (even if they decide not to continue).

Ongoing Training

Earlier we touched on the flawed notion that in coaching or counselling *'one person suffering meets another person who's cured'*. Maintaining strong mental functioning is a life-long pursuit for all of us. In this, the coach / therapist and the coachee / client can be seen as *fellow pilgrims* (Yalom, 1980: 407).

This principle is beautifully illustrated in a story about two famous healers, taken from a book by Hermann Hesse:

> Joseph, one of the healers, severely afflicted with feelings of worthlessness and self-doubt, sets off on a long journey to seek help from his rival, Dion. At an oasis Joseph describes his plight to a stranger, who turns out to be Dion; whereupon Joseph accepts Dion's invitation to go home with him in the role of patient and servant. In time, Joseph regains his former serenity, zest, and effectance and becomes the friend and colleague of his master. Only after many years have passed and Dion lies on his deathbed does he reveal to Joseph that when the latter encountered him at the oasis, he, Dion, had reached a similar impasse in his life and was en route to request Joseph's assistance (1975: 215).

Making a similar point, Hardingham suggests that coaches should be as willing to learn as to teach (1998: 6).

As it's often difficult to determine *a priori* exactly what type of support is needed by clients, it makes sense to find someone who can work at different depths – a person who takes the work seriously enough to have completed a high standard of professional training. My personal belief is that the coach / counsellor needs to have completed significant work *on themselves* to demonstrate humility. While this could be a formal qualification, the requirement that all coaches would go back to college to complete an undergraduate degree in counselling or psychotherapy is unrealistic and probably unnecessary. To overcome this limitation, various mechanisms exist – for example, peer reviews, group therapy, encounter groups and short-duration refresher training. As stated earlier, all of the respondents in this research were professionally trained with a wide range of *routes* being followed – for example, Diplomas in Executive Coaching, courses run by the Psychological Association of Ireland, university programmes and so on. Keeping up-to-date through reading and training (as members of a professional body) seems like a fundamental requirement for anyone who wants to be taken seriously.

The most prominent professional coaching organisations are:

o   Association for Coaching.

o   International Coaching Federation.

o   European Mentoring and Coaching Council.

o   Association of Corporate Executive Coaches.

o   Coaching Network (part of the Psychological Society of Ireland).

Some of these organisations have a formal Continuing Professional Development (CPD) requirement. Some don't. Even those that *push* the CPD requirement struggle to make this mandatory (albeit respondents suggested that this is *becoming* more formal in most of these organisations).

The upside of professional membership includes marketing, ongoing development and access to standard frameworks – for example, codes of ethics. Most of the coaches in this research wanted to see the profession becoming better organised.

Interestingly, all of the therapists met, who also work as coaches, kept accreditation and professional links with their original organisations (British Association of Counselling and Psychotherapy, Centre for Personal Construct Psychology and so on). These organisations typically have a CPD requirement of *circa* 30 hours per year and 'sample the evidence' submitted to keep members on track. In addition, some of these organisations have a requirement of 1+ hours' supervision per month, regardless of the number of clients seen. In effect, these coaches have chosen to impose a higher 'professional standard' on themselves, to differentiate themselves in the marketplace, to *force* themselves to keep abreast of current developments or both.

While it's difficult to prove this point, there also seemed to be a *status issue* at play; coaches with a counselling background wanted to retain the 'badge'. Arguably, being part of an accredited counselling organisation has a higher *cachet* because of the more rigorous entry requirements and elongated training.

Ongoing Supervision

One *test* around CPD is whether the coach is being supervised (counsellors who are part of a professional organisation have no choice, as supervision is a mandatory part of reaccreditation). My personal belief is that all coaches need to be supervised, regardless of depth of experience. Why?

First, for the protection of clients; if there's *something going on* but the coach is not quite sure what to make of it, supervision is the perfect setting to explore this. Second, supervision allows the exploration of transference and counter-transference, the relationship *between* the coach and the coachee. Finally, in order to ensure self-care, coaches need to be aware of their own mental functioning:

> Counsellors can suffer from empathy fatigue. We get moany clients, narcissistic clients and every other label. It's all too easy to burnout. Counsellors should keep a reserve in the tank for themselves (Therapist W).

While the value of supervision was recognised, in the coaching group only 40% of the respondents actually had a supervisor. It may reflect the fact that not all of the people met were full-time coaches (coaching is sometimes run in parallel with a general management consultancy practice). Coaches who are struggling financially may not want to pay for supervision (arguably, a better reason than that they don't believe they *need* it). Yet supervision goes beyond financial considerations and demonstrates humility. Carl Jung declared, "Only the wounded physician heals" (1958: 156) and the eminent Australian psychologist Dorothy Rowe said, "Through our imperfections we help each other" (1994: 15).

It's a privilege to work in a sacred space where people allow us into their lives for a period of time, *swimming alongside* as they progress. To repay that privilege, coaches need to keep their skills at the cutting edge:

> The willingness to work on one's own personality development should not be limited to the training period, but should be viewed as a life task (Lietaer, 1993: 22).

Supervision is a key element in this, both to work on new stuff (continuous learning) and to be reminded of old stuff, staying humble. Shainberg argues that supervision can:

> ... enable the therapists to loosen their deterministic view of the patient as someone different who must be treated with interpretations in order to be healed (1985: 164).

Interpersonal Style

Coaches that communicate *'How I saved the world and other interesting stories'* create a suspicion that they will find it difficult to maximise the potential of the client. If the central role is to unlock potential, can someone with a *me-me-me* communication style actually deliver this?

One suggested *test* under this heading is whether the coach has ever referred a coachee onto someone else. In Ireland, estimates of mental health problems range from one in 10 (College of Psychiatrists, 2013) to one in four of the population (Buckley & Buckley, 2006: 2). If they have an active practice, coaches are therefore likely to encounter serious mental health issues that require specialist treatment – for example, bi-polar or eating disorders. If a coach has *never* referred a coachee to someone else, it *may* signal *arrogance* – the coach doesn't feel that there's any problem they can't tackle personally.

Evaluation Processes

Therapists deem the process to be successful when issues evolve from day-to-day (coping / survival) towards becoming more future-oriented. In the short-term, specific improvements might be around improving relationships or taking less medication. In the medium-term, the goal is often growing independence.

While this outwardly makes sense, none of the therapists met during this research used any formal evaluation methods. Coaches address the evaluation question in a couple of different ways:

> The best form of evaluation is repeat business (Coach O).

> I call clients six months after the assignment ends to see how things have turned out. The feedback at that stage is more valid (Coach L).

Another respondent described evaluation as a form of personal learning:

> I ask for feedback at the end of each assignment. This is as much for my own benefit as I want to keep upping my game (Coach H).

Some of the confusion that exists around evaluation is whether measurement should focus on whether the client *liked* the process or whether it resulted in behavioural change. One respondent said:

> I think most people would find it beneficial to sit in a room with someone – anyone – and be allowed to speak, uninterrupted, for an hour or more whilst an interested, caring person is listening. Is that the same as arguing that 'coaching works'? I don't think so (Purchaser A).

Return on Investment

Evaluation, when it's done at all, is completed with a light touch. Most organisations seem to take a pragmatic stance asking:

- o What did you work on?
- o Did it work out?

Some HR managers use a structured 'checking-in process' – for example, monthly with coachees. At the time of writing, one of the larger financial services organisations was about to launch a pilot evaluation project, working with an academic from Maynooth University (very few organisations in this study had even considered the evaluation question). One respondent described his organisation's philosophy as follows:

> We view coaching the same way that angel investors view emerging companies. You place a range of bets. Not all of them pay off. But, the ones that do, pay off handsomely, covering the costs of the ones that run into the sand (Purchaser D).

Given that the average duration of a coaching assignment was between six and nine months and incurred the high costs detailed earlier, it's surprising that so little effort is placed on evaluation. Yet, when asked if coaching was *'likely to continue to be used in the future',* all of the purchasers answered in the affirmative. While the *science* might be light, there is heavy *support,* a recognition that:

> Coaching and counselling have become firmly established as part of the staff development landscape (Purchaser B).

TERRITORY MAPPING

SKETCHING THE BOUNDARY LINES

In trying to differentiate coaching from counselling, the initial task was to describe each of these practices separately. Sometimes coaching and counselling are described as if they are *unified* fields of practice with agreed methods and standard approaches. The reality is that wide variations exist *within* each discipline. Differences within counselling are well-documented (some of the *schools / approaches* were described earlier). What clearly emerges from this research is the changing nature of coaching. In particular, the movement to therapeutic coaching represents a significant shift from the historical *coach-as-expert* to a non-directive role that sits much closer to counselling. The impact is a 'blurring' of the lines between both disciplines.

Contrasting Approaches

In order to unpack this complex argument, we looked at how each discipline works in practice. The goal was to highlight unique elements in coaching and counselling. We also identified shared or *crossover* practices where the boundary between the disciplines is porous – for example, there are significant differences around timescales. Many of the underpinning theories in counselling were developed by social scientists working with clients over long periods (sometimes several years, involving multiple sessions each week). While 'modern' counselling is seldom as intensive, it can continue for a long period of time. In contrast, the coaching task is to add value in a more restricted timeframe where the 'dosage rate' is significantly lower. Clear differences also emerged around data collection, in the construction of coaching plans and around payment practices. On the question of 'who pays', one respondent suggested that coachees are less committed to the process as they don't use their own money:

> It's like flying business class when the company is picking up the tab. You take it for granted (Coach G).

Yet, despite this outward difference, the 'who pays' question didn't emerge as being particularly important. Executives who enter into a coaching relationship have enormous *'skin in the game'*, even when there's no money involved.

A subtle point here is that while some practices outwardly differ, the impact isn't particularly potent. The Territory Map produced uses a colour-coding scheme to suggest a 'hierarchy of differences' – what's attempted is to demonstrate the *relative importance* of individual elements.

Increasing Overlap

A central finding is the increasing *overlap* between *therapeutic coaching* and *counselling*. Shared elements include *purpose* (maximising potential), *philosophy* (people can 'fix' their own issues), *style of delivery* (non-directive) and the importance of the *relationship* (unconditional positive regard) between client and professional. On the basis of this research, the hypothesis that *coaching and counselling have become blurred and increasingly difficult to disentangle* can be deemed to be *proven*.

The literature review, coupled with the field research, demonstrates confusion among the main players (buyers, coaches, counsellors) about how these practices operate and where boundary lines are drawn.

Outwardly, coaching always *looked like* therapy. Coaches and counsellors both seek to support individuals to make changes in their lives. They are both *delivered* through 'face-to-face' conversations. They both aim to take a person from where they are *today* to a place they want to be at some future point. The incursion of counselling philosophy (being non-directive) and techniques (taking a family history) into coaching, has further *muddied the water*, making it even more difficult to distinguish these practices with any degree of precision.

Coaching Risk

Does it matter? Are these fine line distinctions important? The short answer is *yes*. Understanding the difference between coaching and counselling is extremely important.

Why? Some people present with troubling issues that require deep excavation. While no-one is damaged by being *listened to*, the central risk is that inappropriate or 'surface' *treatment* goes nowhere and people come to believe that their problems are irresolvable. Coaching becomes *'another thing that didn't work'*, with all of the potential negative fallout that can accompany the death of hope.

When commencing my own journey as a newly-minted coach, I was given the advice that coaches should follow the 'rules of surgery': "Don't open something up that you can't stitch back together again". I've now come to believe that this underpinning *fear* places a severe limitation on exploring important issues in depth. Coaches need to know which issues are worth 'staying with' – kept open for longer – despite the discomfort that this can generate. This depth of understanding needs to be coupled with the personal humility to recognise when we are outside our comfort zone – when a coachee requires specialist, therapeutic support that we cannot offer. On the flip-side, coaches bring enormous expertise – around leadership, organisation development, careers and life experience – which can be hugely important and impactful.

The central point is that the roles of coach and therapist are *different*. Neither better, nor worse. Neither superior, nor inferior. Just different.

An understanding of the key differences is required by the players operating in this space if we want to maximise the outcomes for people who seek support. They come with an expectation that we know what we are doing and deserve nothing less.

Coaching Confusion

An important research finding was that the *highest level of confusion* exists in the minds of coaches. The counsellors interviewed seemed clearer and more certain about their role (efficacy arguments about different *types* of therapy continue unabated, but this is a *separate* point).

Two important issues are raised by this. First, to operate in *therapeutic coaching* mode requires considerable professional knowledge and personal skills training. An *understanding* of a specific industry (for example, banking) or the experience of working in a leadership position (for example, as a former CEO) is not enough. The therapeutic coaching model requires in-depth psychological training. This raises significant questions about the accreditation process and the continuous personal development of coaches. Executive coaches are not a homogenous group. Realistically, some won't have the appetite nor the ability to operate in this way. It follows that 'purchasers' need to choose carefully, depending on their exact requirement. Second, in the rush to embrace this 'high-end' form of coaching, the advantages that instructional coaching offers have been overshadowed, even denigrated. There is a continuing useful role for facilitative coaching that incorporates elements of direct training and instruction. Coaches who operate in this domain can be confident about their skills and have no need to feel inferior to those who have chosen a different path.

Of course, the underpinning assumption here is that *all* coaches have enough self-insight to understand strengths and areas into which they shouldn't delve.

Territory Map

In reviewing coaching and counselling practices, Kilburg observed: "the boundaries are not crisply drawn" (2000: 227). The driving focus throughout this research has been to clear the fog that shrouds this topic. The data has allowed the construction of a 'Territory Map' that sets out the *boundaries* between coaching and counselling.

However, one final note of caution needs to be sounded. Any attempt to summarise inevitably simplifies. It is virtually impossible to do justice to the richness of coaching and counselling practices in a short synopsis. The difficulty of accessing actual practice and the relatively small fieldwork sample suggests some caution is required in terms of drawing absolute conclusions. Despite these *caveats*, the territory map detailed over the following pages represents an improvement in our understanding of how coaching and counselling are differentiated and how they overlap. It provides a useful 'starting point' for future research to test the veracity of the points made. I hope that it also provides a roadmap for those considering coaching as a career and inspires you to begin this remarkable journey.

Map Key	
Black *versus* White	Stark differences between Coaching and Counselling.
Dark Grey	Clear differences between Coaching and Counselling.
Light Grey	Some overlap between Coaching and Counselling.
White	Practices virtually indistinguishable or differences are unimportant.

Territory Map: Boundary Lines Between Coaching and Counselling		
	Coaching	Counselling/Therapy
Purpose	Goal-oriented: Help individuals maximise their potential. "You don't have to be sick to get better" (Stewart & Jones, 2012: 296). Coachee does not always arrive with a defined issue (emerges during the process). Some choose coaching as a 'more acceptable' face of therapy - they feel 'shame' or a stigma in going to therapy. Instructional coaching normally leads to a clear result or 'breakthrough'. Therapeutic coaching outcomes are not always as clear-cut.	Therapeutic: Help individuals to improve the quality of their life or to alleviate dysfunction: "... a service sought by people in distress or in some degree of confusion who wish to discuss and resolve these" (Feltham & Dryden, 1993). Client normally arrives with a clear issue. Focus sometimes on diagnostic (presenting issues sometimes labelled as 'pathology'). End result may be better self-regulation (less 'big bang'). Provides hope - change is possible if the client is prepared to work at it (Browne, 2008: 276).

Territory Map: Boundary Lines Between Coaching and Counselling		
	Coaching	Counselling/Therapy
Metaphor	Construction: Action-orientated. Future-focused (historical analysis in some cases). Release the genius that resides within each person. Advance coachee potential.	Renovation: Insight-oriented - new awareness / meaning. Becomes future-focused (often following a new understanding of the past). Repair the damage that has been caused historically (some branches of therapy) and heal emotional wounds.
Assumption	Client may or may not know the solution. Instructional coaching = Doctor / Patient model – for example, training. Normally, coach does not have to be expert in the client's area. Therapeutic coaching has similar assumptions to counselling.	Client 'knows' the solution. A solution imposed by the therapist will not be sustainable and may even be harmful – recreating unhelpful parallels from earlier in the clients' life. Paradoxically, the client may see the therapist as the 'expert' and expect 'analysis', which can cause confusion.
Focus	Work-related: Goal = become more effective in current job or future career. Can be relatively straightforward – for example, acquire a new skill or solve specific problem. Sometimes deals with issues of personal growth - more transformational. Rarely reviews childhood. Focus on conscious thinking.	Work or personal issues: Goal = 'fix' an area that is causing anxiety. Generally, a problem-solving orientation (emotional / behavioural problems or relationship issues). Sometimes existential – for example, becoming the very best version of me. Continually explores childhood and family relationship issues. Focus on unconscious mind (some approaches).
Timeframe	Future Fit: Looking through the windscreen. Assist people to design their future.	Past Experience: Looking through the rear-view mirror to unearth 'hidden tapes' (some branches of therapy do not take this 'historical' route, but most recognise its importance).

Territory Map: Boundary Lines Between Coaching and Counselling		
	Coaching	Counselling/Therapy
Stake-holders	Three or four parties: Coach, coachee, HR, line manager.	Two parties: Client and therapist. Very occasionally link with medical professionals depending on the condition being treated (for example, eating disorders, suicide ideation).
Selection	Organisation: Makes initial 'selection' and then narrows the focus. Coach normally meets coachee for chemistry check. No cost for first meeting.	Client: Hears about counsellor (variety of marketing methods used by therapists). Meet and make a chemistry check decision. Payment normally required for first session.
Contract-ing	Sharing of mutual expectations (process followed, confidentiality, logistics, etc.). Goal = coachee / client will 'take responsibility' for their own issues. Therapists sometimes use test period – for example, four weeks. Issue of 'safety' is stressed across both disciplines – to candidly explore troubling issues with a view to moving forward. Contracts can be written or verbal.	
Relation-ship	High trust = the core relationship issue between the coach / therapist and the coachee / client. This is recognised as centrally important across both therapeutic coaching and counselling (slightly less so in instructional coaching, where the focus is on the 'expertise' of the coach).	
Commit-ment	High personal commitment required from both coachees and counselling clients. This is a difficult journey and the person must be prepared to suffer / invest real energy in the change process.	
Timing	One to two hour sessions (sometimes longer).	55-minute 'hour' sessions are normal.

Territory Map: Boundary Lines Between Coaching and Counselling		
	Coaching	Counselling/Therapy
Duration	Relatively short-term: Often less than six months. 'Dosage' normally between four to eight sessions. Diagnosis, solutions, implementation. Some niche movement towards even more rapid techniques – 'aerobic' coaching. Fast pace.	Relatively long-term: Often more than 12 months. 'Dosage' normally between 12 and 50 sessions. Some movement towards 'brief therapy' (for example, small, fixed number of sessions in CBT) often driven by cost considerations of external providers – for example, health insurers / EAP providers. Slow pace.
Modality	Range of methods: Face-to-face, telephone, email, Skype or some combination of methods.	Single method: Generally face-to-face only. Concern around 'missing' communication signals or not being fully able to contain client anxieties.
Payee	The organisation: Coach has a dual loyalty (to coachee and the organisation).	The client (sometimes health insurers): Therapist has a single loyalty (to the client).
Cost	Range = €125 to €350 per hour (sometimes higher than this).	Range = €50 to €70 per hour.

Territory Map: Boundary Lines Between Coaching and Counselling		
	Coaching	Counselling/Therapy
Role	Varies: Ranges from 'telling' (instructional coaching) that includes content inputs. Pragmatic - 'get it fixed'. Advice is given if the coach is knowledgeable in a particular area and the client requests this. Can also be more facilitative (therapeutic model is very similar to counselling).	Focused: Non-advisory and non-directional are cornerstones. Major focus on 'process' rather than content. Some clients have an expectation that sessions will be 'directional' and are disappointed. Some schools of counselling are more directive than others – for example, CBT (the term 'directive' is generally not 'PC'). Structured approaches where the client is essentially 'instructed' to follow a particular set of activities are normally referred to as 'collaborative', a misnomer as all counselling has a collaborative orientation).
Style	Idiosyncratic: Dependant on the background / training of the individual coach and personal style - movement to positive psychology (what energises and drives people forward rather than what causes pain). Can be radically different – for example, 'here's how to do that' *versus* 100% non-directive. Can sometimes create chaos / controlled instability to promote coachee's growth (Cavanagh, 2005).	Similar: Also dependant on the background / training of the individual therapist. Can be radically different – for example, psychodynamic approach uncovers behavioural patterns through personal history taking and focusing on the role of the unconscious *versus* Gestalt, which focuses on 'what's happening 'here-and-now'. Positive psychology movement has shifted attention from pathology model. Physical movements – for example, art therapy - is very different to anything used in coaching. General emphasis = reduce 'life crisis'.

Territory Map: Boundary Lines Between Coaching and Counselling		
	Coaching	Counselling/Therapy
Diagnosis	Data: Explicit data collection phase. May involve others – for example, 360⁰ feedback, telephone interviews or the use of psychometrics. Sometimes diagnosis is supplied by the employer. Can involve 'shadowing' - the coach works alongside the coachee in a work setting.	Data: Collection conducted by the therapist one-on-one. Private process. Very little use of 'instruments'. 'Thinking' subsequently made known to the client through the use of questions / Interventions posed by the therapist. Therapist seldom accompanies the client (exception = behaviour modification in the treatment of some phobias).
Feedback	Goal = create awareness: formal coaching plan developed. Cards played 'face up'. Some coaches don't produce documentation and work without notes. Slightly more challenge because of different training and shorter timeframes.	Goal = create awareness (similar). However, diagnosis is often 'in the mind' of the therapist and emerges during discussion. No transfer of 'notes' or written materials (therapist keeps own notes, normally written immediately after each session; reviewed prior to next session).
Self-reveal	Frequently: As a way to demonstrate a practice or offer a model for the coachee to follow. Generally more personal disclosure by a coach (as an aid to learning).	Exceptionally: Only as a way of allowing the client to know that s/he has been understood. Normally very limited disclosure.
Place	Variety of locations: Client's place of work, the coach's office or a neutral venue - coaching over lunch.	Conducted at therapist's office: (exception = some phobias treated externally). Key concern = I am not the client's 'friend' (meeting outside of a therapy setting risks blurring this boundary line).

Territory Map: Boundary Lines Between Coaching and Counselling		
	Coaching	Counselling/Therapy
Home-work	Yes: Coachees may be asked to complete specific tasks (for example, structured exercises) or experiments and report back. Homework used to speed up the process and make better use of time. Contact 'between' the sessions to communicate 'wins'.	No: Generally, no homework (other than thinking about what happened during the session). Some schools use homework – for example, CBT therapists asking clients to record levels of anxiety or depression. Contact 'between' the sessions normally only used in cases of difficulty or crisis.
Complet-ion	Normally completed: Programmes are normally closed out (unless circumstances in the organisation change).	Range of endings: Clients don't always stay for a variety of reasons (duration, slow pace of progress, cost, difficult issues raised in the process).
Credent-ials	Unregulated: No formal accreditation. Mix of backgrounds (business and psychology predominate). No standardised training route. Coaching clients not seen as 'vulnerable' and don't need 'protection'.	More regulated: Norm = formal training in one of the 'schools' of therapy. Must be qualified to practice using the term 'psychotherapist'. Minimum of three years' study followed by accreditation process. However, there is no formal regulation of counsellors in Ireland at the time of writing.
Ongoing Training	Some: Membership of coaching bodies is voluntary and seldom sought by buyers (changing somewhat). No formal supervision (some coaches opt for this voluntarily). 'Lowish' CPD training requirement.	More: Work to a defined CPD structure with ongoing supervision (often on an 10:1 basis - 1 supervised session for every 10 client meetings). Re-accreditation every five years. Not possible to work as a non-accredited counsellor (due to need to secure insurance).
Outcome 1	Learning - for example, a new skill or self-insight.	Learning - for example, self-insight / discovery.
Outcome 2	Stimulate new actions. Maximise potential.	Ameliorate dysfunction. Maximise potential.

Territory Map: Boundary Lines Between Coaching and Counselling		
	Coaching	Counselling/Therapy
Outcome 3	Few measures: Self-reporting by clients. Sometimes evaluation completed by HR to assess effectiveness. 'Before & after' 360^0 measurements used in minority of organisations. Concern = passing trend - 'No evidence, no advocates' (Feldman & Lankau, 2005).	Less measures: No formal measurements other than client feedback: "Have the presenting issues gone away?", "Do I feel better?" The absence of measurement does not imply that counselling lacks impact - it can have enormous punch – for example, in terms of self-acceptance (Dougherty & West, 2007).
Outcome 4	Additional possibilities: Achievement of coaching objectives, coach feedback, staff retention, coach performance (various issues – for example, accurate billing), employee engagement surveys and improved performance ratings. Central point is not the difficulty of developing a dashboard, but how little effort is normally made to quantify the benefits.	
Does it work?	Outcomes vary: Not all coachees / clients benefit. Some need deeper psychiatric intervention to deal with interpersonal problems or psychopathology. Some are 'immune' to change and resist feedback. Sometimes a crisis emerges mid-therapy and the coachee / client leaves. The cost of programmes also can be prohibitive. Some coaches and therapists are simply not effective - the coachee / client doesn't feel they have the ability to 'crack the code'.	

REFERENCES

American Counseling Association (1997). *Code of Ethics & Professional Standards*, Alexandria, VA: American Counseling Association.

American Counseling Association (2007). *Code of Ethics & Professional Standards*, Alexandria, VA: American Counseling Association.

Anderson, M. (2001). *Executive Briefing: Case study on the Return on Investment of Executive Coaching*, http://www.metrixglobal.net.

Anderson, V., Rayner, C. & Schyns, B. (2009*). Coaching at the Sharp End: The Role of Line Managers in Coaching at Work*, London: Chartered Institute of Personnel & Development.

Argyris, C. (1990). *Overcoming Organizational Defenses: Facilitating Organisation Learning*, Englewood Cliffs, NJ: Prentice Hall.

Auerbach, E. (2006). 'Cognitive Coaching' in Stober, D. & Grant, A. (Eds.), *Evidence-Based Coaching Handbook*, New York: Wiley.

Barrett-Leonard, G. (1962) 'Dimensions of a Therapist Response as Causal Factors in Therapeutic Change', *Psychological Monographs*, Vol.76 (43, Whole No.562).

Bateman, A. & Holmes, J. (1995). *Introduction to Psychoanalysis*, London: Routledge.

Beebe, B. & Lachmann, F. (2002). *Infant Research and Adult Treatment: Co-Constructing Interaction*, Hillsdale, NJ: Analytic Press.

Beisser, A. (1970). 'The Paradoxical Theory of Change' in Fagin, J. & Shepherd, I. (Eds.), *Gestalt Therapy Now*, pp.77-80, New York: Harper and Row.

Berglas, S. (2002). 'The Very Real Dangers of Executive Coaching'. *Harvard Business Review*, Vol.80, June, pp.86-93.

Berne, E. (1964). *Games People Play: The Psychology of Human Relationships*, New York: Ballantine Books.

Bluckert, P. (2006). *Psychological Dimensions of Executive Coaching*, New York: McGraw-Hill.

Bok, D. (1986). *Higher Learning*, Cambridge, MA: Harvard University Press.

Booth, W., Colomb, G. & Williams J. (2008). *The Craft of Research*, Chicago: University of Chicago Press.

Bowlby, J. (1953). *Maternal Care and the Growth of Love*, Harmondsworth: Penguin Books.

Bowlby, J. (1969). *Attachment and Loss: Volume 1*, New York: Basic Books.

British Association for Counselling (BAC) (1986). *Counselling: Definition of Terms in use with Expansion and Rationale (Information Sheet 1)*, Rugby: British Association for Counselling.

Brookfield, S. (1986). *Understanding and Facilitating Adult Learning*, Buckingham: Open University Press.

Brotman, L., Liberi, W. & Wasylyshyn, K. (1998). 'Executive Coaching: The Need For Standards of Competence', *Consulting Psychology Journal: Practice and Research*, Vol.50, pp.40-46.

Browne, I. (2008). *Music and Madness*, Cork: Atrium.

Buber, M. (1967). *A Believing Humanism: Gleanings*, New York: Simon & Schuster.

Buckley, A. & Buckley, C. (2006). *A Guide to Coaching and Mental Health*, Abingdon: Routledge.

Burn, G. (Ed.) (2007). *Personal Development All-in-One for Dummies*, Chichester: John Wiley & Sons.

Camerer, C. (1997). 'Progress In Behavioural Game Theory', *Journal of Economic Perspectives*, Vol.11, No.4, pp.167-188.

Casey, J. (1996). 'Gail F. Farwell: A Developmentalist Who Lives His Ideas', *The School Counsellor*, Vol.43, pp.174-180.

Cavanagh, M. (2003). 'Coaching From a Systemic Perspective: A Complex Adaptive Approach' in Stober, D. & Grant, A. (Eds.), *Evidence-Based Coaching Handbook*, New York: Wiley.

Cavanagh, M. (2005). 'Mental-Health Issues and Challenging Clients in Executive Coaching' in Cavanagh, M., Grant A. & Kemp T. (2005), *Evidence-Based Coaching: Theory, Research and Practice From The Behavioural Sciences*, Samford Valley, QLD: Australian Academic Press.

Cavanagh, M. (2006). 'Coaching from a Systemic Perspective: A Complex, Adaptive Conversation', in Stober, D. & Grant, A. (Eds.), *Evidence Based Coaching Handbook: Putting Best Practices to Work for Your Clients*, New York: Wiley.

Cavanagh, M., Grant A. & Kemp T. (2005),.*Evidence-Based Coaching: Theory, Research and Practice From The Behavioural Sciences*, Samford Valley, QLD: Australian Academic Press.

Chapman, M. (2006). Quoted in Jarvis, J., Lane, D. & Fillery-Travis, A. (2006), *The Case for Coaching*, London: Chartered Institute of Personnel and Development.

Chartered Institute of Personnel & Development (CIPD) (2009). *Taking the Temperature of Coaching*, London: Chartered Institute of Personnel and Development.

College of Psychiatrists (2013). *Pre-Budget 2014 Submission regarding Mental Health Services*, Dublin: College of Psychiatrists, September 2013.

Copeland, M. (2005). *Socratic Circles: Fostering Critical and Creative Thinking*, Portland, MN: Stenhouse Publishers.

Corbett, B. & Colemon, J. (2005). *The Sherpa Guide: Process-Driven Executive Coaching*, Boston, MA: Cengage Learning.

Corporate Leadership Council (2003). Maximizing Returns on Professional Executive Coaching. Washington, DC: Corporate Leadership Council.

Coutu, D. & Kauffman, C. (2009). 'What Can Coaches Do For You?', *Harvard Business Review*, January.

Cox, E., Bachkirova, T. & Clutterbuck, D. (Eds.) (2014). The Complete Handbook of Coaching (2nd Edition), London: SAGE Publications.

Cozolino, L. (2004). *The Making of a Therapist*, New York: W.W. Norton.

De Meuse, K., Guangrong, D. & Lee, R.J. (2009). 'Evaluating the Effectiveness of Executive Coaching: Beyond ROI?', *Coaching: An International Journal of Theory, Research and Practice*, Vol.2, No.2 (Sept.), pp.117-134.

Dougherty, N. & West, J. (2007). *The Matrix and Meaning of Character: An Archetypal and Developmental Approach*, Abingdon: Routledge.

Drake, D. (2009). 'Using Attachment *Theory in Coaching Leaders: The Search for a Coherent Narrative'*, *International Coaching Psychology Review*, Vol.41, No.1, pp.49-58.

Druckman, D. & Bjork, R. (1991). *In the Mind's Eye: Enhancing Human Performance,* Washington DC: National Academy Press.

Evered, R. & Selman, J. (1989). 'Coaching and the Art of Management', *Organizational Dynamics*, Vol.18, pp.16-32.

Eysenck, H. (1957). Sense and Nonsense in Psychology, Harmondsworth: Penguin Books.

Feldman, D. (1999). 'Toxic Mentors or Toxic Protégés? A Critical Re-examination of Dysfunctional Mentoring', *Human Resource Management Review*, Vol.9, pp.247-278.

Feldman, D. & Lankau, M. (2005). 'Executive Coaching: A Review and Agenda for Future Research', *Journal of Management*, Vol.31, pp.828-848.

Feltham, C. & Dryden, W. (1993). Dictionary of Counselling, London: Wiley-Blackwell.

Filipczak, B. (1998). 'The Executive Coach: Helper or Healer?', *Training*, Vol.35, No.3, pp.30-36.

Freud, S. (1905). *On Psychotherapy*, London: Hogarth Press.

Freud, S. (1940). *An Outline of Psychoanalysis*, London: Hogarth Press.

Gallwey, T. (2010). The Inner Game of Coaching, Stauffen, Germany: Allesimfluss-Verlag.

Gegner, C. (1997). 'Coaching: Theory and Practice', unpublished Master's Thesis, University of San Francisco, California.

Gendlin, E. (1968). 'The Experiential Response' in Hammer, E. (Ed.), *Use of Interpretation in Therapy: Technique and Art*, pp.208-227, New York: Grune & Stratton.

Gill, J. & Johnson, P. (2010). *Research Methods for Managers*, London: Sage.

Goldsmith, M. (2008). *What Got You Here Won't Get You There*, London: Profile Books.

Goleman, D. (2007). *Social Intelligence*, London: Arrow Books.

Grant, A. (2003). 'The Impact of Life Coaching on Goal Attainment, Metacognition and Mental Health', *Social Behaviour and Personality*, Vol.31, No.3, pp.253-264.

Grant, A. (2008). 'Past Present and Future: The Evolution of Professional Coaching and Coaching Psychology' in Palmer, S. & Whybrow, A. (Eds.), *Handbook of Coaching Psychology*, London: Routledge.

Grant, A. & Cavanagh, M. (2004). 'Towards a Profession of Coaching: Sixty-Five Years of Progress and Challenges for the Future', *International Journal of Evidence-Based Coaching and Mentoring*, Vol.2, No.1, pp.1-16.

Grant, A. & Stober, D. (2006). *Evidence-Based Coaching Handbook*, New York: Wiley.

Grant, A. & Zackon, R. (2004). 'Executive, Workplace and Life Coaching: Findings From a Large-Scale Survey on International Coach Federation Members', *International Journal of Evidence-Based Coaching and Mentoring*, Vol.2, No.2, pp.1-15.

Gray, D. (2006). 'Executive Coaching: Towards a Dynamic Alliance of Psychotherapy and Transformative Learning Processes', *Management Learning*, Vol.37, No.4, pp.475-497.

Grimley, B. (2008). 'NLP Coaching' in Palmer, S. & Whybrow A. (Eds.), *Handbook of Coaching Psychology*, London: Routledge.

Hall, D., Otazo, K. & Hollenbeck, G. (1999). 'Behind Closed Doors: What Really Happens in Executive Coaching?', *Organisation Dynamics*, Vol.28, pp.39-53.

Hardingham, A. (1998). *Psychology for Trainers*, London: Chartered Institute of Personnel & Development.

Harris, M. (1999). 'Look, it's a Psychologist ... no, it's a Trainer ... no, it's an Executive Coach', *TIP*, Vol.36, No.3, pp.1-5.

Harris, T. (1969). *I'm OK, You're OK*, New York: Harper-Row.

Hesse, H. (1975). Quoted in Yalom, I. (1980). *Existential Psychotherapy*, New York: Basic Books.

Hollis, J. (2005). *Finding Meaning in the Second Half of Life*, New York: Penguin Books.

Horvat, A. & Greenberg, L. (1994). *The Working Alliance: Theory, Research and Practice*, New York: John Wiley & Sons.

Hycner, R. (1998). *Between Person and Person*, Highland, NY: Gestalt Journal Publications.

Ives, Y. (2008). 'What is 'Coaching?' An Exploration of Conflicting Paradigms', *International Journal of Evidence-Based Coaching and Mentoring*, Vol.6, No.2 (Aug.), pp.100-113.

Jarvis, J., Lane, D. & Fillery-Travis, A. (2006). *The Case for Coaching*, London: Chartered Institute of Personnel and Development.

Judge, W. & Cowell, J. (1997). 'The Brave New World of Executive Coaching', *Business Horizons*, Vol.4, No.40.

Jung, C. (1958). *Memories, Dreams, Reflections*, London: Fontana Press.

Kahn, M. (1997). *Between Therapist and Client*, New York: W.H. Freeman & Company.

Kauffman, C. (2006). 'Positive Psychology: The Science at the Heart of Coaching' in Stober, D. & Grant A. (Eds.), *Evidence-Based Coaching Handbook*, Hoboken, NJ: Wiley.

Kauffman, C. & Scouler, A. (2004). 'Towards a Positive Psychology of Executive Coaching' in Lindley, P. & Joseph, S. (Eds.), *Positive Psychology in Practice*, pp. 335-353, Hoboken, NJ: Wiley.

Kaufman, B. (2006). 'The Role of Executive Coaching in Performance Management', *Handbook of Business Strategy*, Vol,7, No.1, pp.287-291.

Keddy, J. & Johnson, C. (2011). *Managing Coaching at Work*, London: Kogan Page.

Kegan, R. (1998). *In Over Our Heads: The Mental Demands of Modern Life*, Cambridge, MA: Harvard University Press.

Kegan, R. & Lahey, L. (2001). *How the Way We Talk Can Change the Way We Work*, San Francisco: Jossey-Bass.

Kegan, R. & Lahey, L. (2009). *Immunity to Change*, Cambridge, MA: Harvard Business School Publishing.

Kelly, G. (1991). *The Psychology of Personal Constructs: Volumes 1 and 2*, London: Routledge (in association with the Centre for Personal Construct Psychology). Originally Published in 1951.

Kelly, W. (1971). *Pogo*, New York: Post-Hall Syndicate.

Kiel, R., Rimmer, E., Williams, K. & Doyle, M. (1996). 'Coaching At The Top', *Consulting Psychology Journal: Practice and Research*, Vol.48, pp.67-77.

Kilburg, R. (1996). 'Executive Coaching as an Emerging Competency in the Practice of Consultation', *Consulting Psychology Journal: Practice and Research*, Vol.48, pp.59-60.

Kilburg, R. (1997). 'Coaching and Executive Character: Core Problems and Basic Approaches', *Consulting Psychology Journal: Practice and Research*, Vol.49, pp.281-299.

Kilburg, R. (2000). *Executive Coaching: Developing Managerial Wisdom in a World of Chaos*, Washington DC: American Psychological Association.

Kirschembaum, H. & Land-Henderson, V. (1990). *The Carl Rogers Reader*, Boston: Hougton Mifflin Company.

Kneebone, R., Kidd, J., Nestel, D., Asvall, S., Paraskeva, P. & Darzi, A. (2002). 'An Innovative Model For Teaching and Learning Clinical Procedures', *Medical Education*, Vol.36, No.7 (July), pp.628-634.

Krishnamurti, J. (1991). *Commentaries On Living: Third Series*, London: Victor Gollancz.

Latham, G., Almost, J., Mann, S. & Moore, C. (2005). 'New Developments in Performance Management', *Organisation Dynamics*, Vol.34, No.1, pp.78-87.

Lee, G. (2003). *Leadership Coaching: From Personal Insight to Organisational Performance*, London: Chartered Institute of Personnel & Development.

Lee, G. (2009). 'The Psychodynamic Approach to Coaching' in Cox, E., Bachkirova, T. & Clutterbuck, D. (Eds.), *The Complete Handbook of Coaching*, pp. 23-36. London: Sage Publications.

Levinson, H. (1996). 'Executive Coaching', *Consulting Psychology Journal: Practice and Research*, Vol.48, pp.115-123.

Lietaer, G. (1993). 'Authenticity, Congruence and Transparency' in Brazier, D. (Ed.). *Beyond Carl Rogers*, pp.17-46, London: Constable.

Liljenstrand, A. & Nebeker, D. (2008). 'Coaching Services: A Look At Coaches, Clients and Practices', *Consulting Psychology Journal: Practice & Research*, Vol.60, pp.57 -77.

Lindley, P., Joseph, S., Harrington, S. & Wood, A. (2006). 'Positive Psychology: Past, Present and (Possible) Future', *The Journal of Positive Psychology*, Vol.1, No.1, pp.3-16.

Linley, P. & Harrington, S. (2008). 'Integrating Positive Psychology and Coaching Psychology: Shared Assumptions and Aspirations?' in Palmer, S. & Whybrow, A. (Eds.), *Handbook of Coaching Psychology*, London: Routledge.

Locke, E. & Latham, G. (1990). *A Theory of Goal Setting and Task Performance*, Englewood Cliffs, NJ: Prentice-Hall.

London, M. (2002). *Leadership Development: Paths to Self-Insight and Professional Growth*, Mahwah, NJ: Lawrence Erlbaum.

Lukaszewski, J. (1988). 'Behind The Throne: How To Coach and Counsel Executives', *Training and Development Journal*, Vol.42, No.10, pp.33-35.

Mackewn, J. (1997). *Developing Gestalt Counselling*, London: Sage Publications.

MacKie, D. (2007). 'Evaluating the Effectiveness of Executive Coaching: Where Are We Now And Where Do We Need To Be?', *Australian Psychologist*, Vol.42, pp.310 -318.

Maslow, A. (1954). *Motivation and Personality*, New York: Harper & Row Publishers.

McGeever, M. (2010). 'Power Music' in McMahon, G. & Archer, A. (Eds.), *101 Coaching Strategies and Techniques*, pp. 28-30, London: Routledge.

McGoldrick, M., Gerson, R. & Petry, S. (2008). *Genograms: Assessment and Intervention* (3rd Edition), New York: Norton Professional Books.

McGovern, J., Lindemann, M., Vergara, M., Murphy, S., Barker, L. & Warrenfeltz, R. (2001). 'Maximizing the Impact of Executive Coaching: Behavioural Change, Organisational Outcomes, and Return on Investment', *Manchester Review*, Vol.6, No.1, p.1 9.

McLean, G. & Kuo, M. (2000). 'Coaching in Organizations: Self-Assessment of Competence' in Kuchinke, K. (Ed.), *Proceedings of The Academy of Human Resource Development Conference*, Raleigh-Durham, Morrisville, NC, pp. 638-645.

McMahon, G. & Archer A. (2010). *101 Coaching Strategies and Techniques*, London: Routledge.

McNutt, R. & Wright, P. (1995). 'Coaching Your Employees: Applying Sports Analogies To Business', *Executive Development*, Vol.8, No.1, pp.27-32.

Mearns, D. (1994). *Developing Person-Centered Counselling*, London: Sage Publications.

Mearns, D. & Thorne, B. (1988). *Person-Centered Counselling in Action*, London: Sage Publications.

Mearns, D., Thorne, B. & McLeod, J. (2013). *Person-Centered Counselling in Action*, London: Sage Publications.

Miller, W. & Rollnick, S. (2002). *Motivational Interviewing: Preparing People for Change* (2nd Edition), New York: Guildford Press.

Milner, J., Ostmeier, E. & Franke, R. (2013). 'Critical Incidents in Cross-cultural Coaching: The View from German Coaches', *International*

Journal of Evidence Based Coaching and Mentoring, Vol.11, No.2, pp.19-32.

Mooney, P. (2008). *Desperate Executives: A Story of Coaching, Change and Personal Growth*, Dublin: The Liffey Press.

Mooney, P. (2009). *Accidental Leadership: A Personal Journey*, Dublin: The Liffey Press.

Mooney, P. (2012). *The Transformation Roadmap: Accelerating Organisation Change*, Cork: Oak Tree Press.

Naughton, J. (2002). 'The Coaching Boom: Is it the Long-Awaited Alternative to the Medical Model?', *Psychotherapy Networker*, No.42 (July/Aug.), pp.1-10.

Nelson-Jones, R. (2000). *Six Key Approaches to Counselling & Therapy*, London: Continuum.

Noer, D. (2000). 'The Big Three Derailment Factors in a Coaching Relationship' in Goldsmith, M., Lyons, L. & Freas, A. (Eds.), *Coaching For Leadership: How the World's Greatest Coaches Help Leaders Learn*, pp.317-324, San Francisco: Jossey-Bass.

Nowers, M. (2006). 'Foreword' in Buckley, A. & Buckley, C. (2006). *A Guide to Coaching and Mental Health*, London: Routledge.

O'Brien, M. (1997). 'Executive Coaching', *Supervision*, Vol.58, No.4, pp.6-8.

Olivero, G., Bane, K. & Kopelman, R. (1997) 'Executive Coaching as a Transfer of Training Tool: Effects on Productivity in a Public Agency', *Public Personnel Management*, Vol.26, No.4, pp.464-469.

Palmer, S. & Szymanska, K. (2008). 'Cognitive Behavioural Coaching: An Integrative Approach' in Palmer, S. & Whybrow, A. (Eds.), *Handbook of Coaching Psychology*, London: Routledge.

Palmer, S. & Whybrow, A. (Eds.) (2008). *Handbook of Coaching Psychology*, London: Routledge.

Paris, G. (2007). *Wisdom of the Psyche: Depth Psychology After Neuroscience*, London: Routledge.

Parsloe, E. & Wray, M. (2000). *Coaching and Mentoring*, London: Kogan Page.

Passmore, J. & Whybrow, A. (2008). 'Motivational Interviewing: A Specific Approach for Coaching Psychologists' in Palmer, S. & Whybrow, A. (Eds.), *Handbook of Coaching Psychology*, London: Routledge.

Pelham, G. (2014). Unpublished book chapters, *UCD Student Handbook*.

Peltier, B. (2001). *The Psychology of Executive Coaching: Theory and Application*, London: Brunner-Routledge.

Peltier, B. (2009). *The Psychology of Executive Coaching: Theory and Application* (2nd Edition), London: Routledge.

Perls, F., Hefferline, R. & Goodman, P. (1994). *Gestalt Therapy, Excitement and Growth in Human Personality*, New York: Gestalt Journal Press.

Perry, B., Pollard, R., Blakely, T., Baker, W. & Vigilante, D. (1995). 'Childhood Trauma, the Neurobiology of Adaptation and Use-Dependant Development of the Brain: How 'States' Become 'Traits', *Infant Mental Health Journal*, Vol.16, No.4, pp.271-291.

Peterson, C. (2000). 'The Future of Optimism', *American Psychologist*, Vol.55, pp.44-55.

Peterson, D. (2002). 'Management Development: Coaching and Mentoring Programs' in Kraiger, K. (Ed.), *Creating, Implementing, and Managing Effective Training and Development*, pp. 160 -191, San Francisco: Jossey-Bass.

Price, J. (2009). 'The Coaching / Therapy Boundary in Organizational Coaching', *Coaching: An International Journal of Theory, Research and Practice*, Vol.2, No.2, pp.135-148.

Prochaska, J. & Norcross, J. (2001). 'Stages of Change', *Psychotherapy*, Vol.38, No.4, pp.443-448.

Purcell, J., Kinnie, N., Hutchinson, S. & Swart, J. (2003). *Understanding the People and Performance Link: Unlocking the Black Box*, London: Chartered Institute of Personnel & Development.

Ragins, B., Cotton, J. & Miller, J. (2000). 'Marginal Mentoring: The Effects of Type of Mentor, Quality of Relationship, and Program Design on Work and Career Related Attitudes', *Academy of Management Journal*, Vol.43, pp.1177-1194.

Reams, J. (2009). 'Immunity to Change: A Report From the Field', *Integral Review*, Vol.5, June, pp.170-182.

Rogers, C. (1951). *Client-Centered Therapy*, Boston: Houghton Mifflin.

Rogers, C. (1957). 'The Necessary and Sufficient Conditions of Therapeutic Personality Change', *Journal of Consulting Psychology*, Vol.21, pp.95-103.

Rogers, C. (1967). *The Therapeutic Relationship and its Impact: A Study of Psychotherapy with Schizophrenics*, Madison, WI: University of Wisconsin Press.

Rogers, J. (2011). 'Foreword' in Sandler, C. (2011). *Executive Coaching: A Psychodynamic Approach*, Buckingham: Open University Press.

Rowe, D. (1994). *Beyond Fear*, London: Harper-Collins.

Sandler, C. (2011). *Executive Coaching: A Psychodynamic Approach*, Buckingham: Open University Press.

Sandler, C. (2012). Interview conducted in *Coaching Today*, October.

Saporito, T. (1996). 'Business-Linked Executive Development: Coaching Senior Executives', *Research*, Vol.48, pp.96-103.

Scandura, T. (1998). 'Dysfunctional Mentoring Relationships and Outcomes', *Journal of Management*, Vol.24, pp.449-467.

Schutzenberger, A. (1991). 'The Drama of the Seriously Ill Patient: Fifteen Years' Experience of Psychodrama and Cancer' in Holmes, P. & and Karp, M. (Eds.), *Psychodrama: Inspiration and Technique*, London: Routledge.

Seligman, M. & Csikszentmihalyi, M. (2000). 'Positive Psychology: An Introduction', *American Psychologist*, Vol.55, No.1, pp.5-14.

Shainberg, D. (1985). 'Teaching Therapists How To Be With Their Clients' in Welwood, J., *Awakening the Heart: East / West Approaches to Psychotherapy and the Healing Relationship*, Boston & London: Shambhala.

Sheppard, G. (2004). 'What is Counselling? A Search for a Definition' in Gladding, S. (2004), *Counselling: A Comprehensive Profession* (5th Edition), Upper Saddle River, NJ: Merrill / Prentice-Hall.

Smith, L. (1993). 'The Executive's New Coach', *Fortune*, Vol.128, No.16, pp.126-134.

Smither, J. (2011). 'Can Psychotherapy Research Serve as a Guide for Research about Executive Coaching? An Agenda for the Next Decade', *Journal of Business Psychology*, Vol.26, pp.135-145.

Snyder, C. & McCullough, M. (2000). 'A Positive Psychology Field of Dreams: If You Build It They Will Come', *Journal of Social & Clinical Psychology*, Vol.19, No.1, pp.151-160.

Sperry, L. (1993). 'Working with Executives: Consulting, Counseling, and Coaching', *Individual Psychology*, Vol.49, No.2, pp.257-266.

Spinelli, E. & Horner, C. (2008). 'Existential Approach to Coaching Psychology' in Palmer, S. & Whybrow, A. (Eds.), *Handbook of Coaching Psychology*, London & New York: Routledge.

Stewart, I. & Jones, V. (2012). *TA Today – A New Introduction to Transactional Analysis* (2nd Edition), Derby: Lifespace Publishing.

Stober, D. & Grant, A. (2006). 'Towards a Contextual Approach to Coaching Models' in Stober, D. & Grant, A. (Eds.), *Evidence-Based Coaching Handbook*, New York: Wiley.

Stojnov, D. & Pavlovic, J. (2010). 'An Invitation to Personal Construct Coaching: From Personal Construct Therapy to Personal Construct Coaching', *International Coaching Psychology Review*, Vol.5, No.2 (Sept.).

Summerfield, J. (2002). 'Walking the Thin Line: Coaching or Counselling?', *Training Journal*, Nov., pp.36-39.

Summerfield, J. (2006). 'Do We Coach or Do We Counsel? Thoughts on the 'Emotional Life' of a Coaching Session', *The Coaching Psychologist*, Vol.2, No.1 (May).

Tobias, L. (1996). 'Coaching Executives', *Consulting Psychology Journal: Practice and Research*, Vol.48, No.2, pp.87-95.

Valerio, A. & Lee, R. (2005). *Executive Coaching: A Guide for the HR Professional*, San Francisco: Pfeiffer.

Van Deurzen, E. (2002). *Existential Counselling & Psychotherapy in Practice*, London: Sage Publications.

Van Velsor, E. & Guthrie, V. (1998). 'Enhancing The Ability to Learn From Experience' in McCauley, C., Moxley, R. & Van Velsor, E. (Eds.), *The Center for Creative Leadership Handbook of Leadership Development*, San Francisco: Jossey-Bass.

Vicere, A. & Fulmer, R. (1996). *Crafting Competitiveness: Developing Leaders in the Shadow Pyramid*, Oxford: Capstone Publishing.

West, L. & Milan, M. (Eds.) (2001). *The Reflecting Glass*, London: Palgrave.

Whitmore, J. (2009). *Coaching for Performance* (4th Edition), London: Nicholas Brealey Publishing.

Whybrow, A. & Palmer, S. (2006). 'Taking Stock: A Survey of Coaching Psychologists' Practices and Perspectives', *International Coaching Psychology Review*, Vol.1, No.1, pp.56-70.

Wilkins, P. (2000). 'Unconditional Positive Regard Reconsidered', *British Journal of Guidance & Counselling*, Vol.28, No.1, pp.23-37.

Williams, P. (2003). 'The Potential Perils of Personal Issues in Coaching: The Continuing Debate: Therapy or Coaching?', *International Journal of Coaching in Organizations*, Vol.2, No.2, pp.21-30.

Witherspoon, R. & White, R. (1996). 'Executive Coaching: A Continuum of Roles', *Consulting Psychology Journal: Practice and Research*, Vol.48, pp.124-133.

Yalom, I. (1975). *Theory and Practice of Group Psychotherapy*, New York: Basic Books.

Yalom, I. (1980). *Existential Psychotherapy*, New York: Basic Books.

Yalom, I. (2005). *The Schopenhauer Cure*, New York: HarperCollins.

APPENDIX A: RESEARCH METHODOLOGY

Semi-Structured Interviews: A series of semi-structured interviews with specialists in the coaching and counselling arena was deemed the optimum approach. This qualitative bias (conducting face-to-face meetings rather than distributing questionnaires or conducting online surveys) yielded a rich stream of information. The hypothesis was not revealed to the group interviewed, avoiding any potential 'response bias'. While I've worked as an executive coach for many years, I'm not an accredited counsellor. Therefore the arguments around counselling must be tempered by the fact that my understanding has been gleaned from the literature review and the interviews conducted with therapists, rather than personal experience.

Standardised Questionnaires: The questionnaires used were piloted with a small number of respondents. Several changes were needed in the phrasing of questions to make the intent clearer and some extraneous questions were deleted (see questionnaires below). The length and scope of these was an early hurdle, particularly around the level of detail needed. As the duration of interviews was a constraint, a balance had to be struck between comprehensiveness and *testing the patience* of respondents. On reflection, there were too many questions and the full list was only completed in about 66% of cases. The questionnaire was sent to respondents in advance of our meeting, allowing them time to think about the topics posed. In 33% of cases, the respondents sent a written response to the questions (one of the options provided).

Sample Size: Given the research timescale, how many people should be interviewed? There were potentially six separate 'groups' that could usefully contribute to this research:

o **Group 1:** Purchasers of executive coaching: 4 people.
o **Group 2:** Purchasers of counselling: 2 people.
o **Group 3:** Executive coaching practitioners: 12 people.
o **Group 4:** Counsellors and psychotherapists: 6 people.
o **Group 5:** Coachees: Users of executive coaching.

o **Group 6:** Clients: Users of counselling services.

Narrowing the Scope: I considered 'sitting in' on coaching or counselling meetings and observing what happens first-hand. Even assuming that I could get coaches / counsellors to agree, the difficulty in explaining this to their clients posed a hurdle along with the possible downside of the *Hawthorne Effect* with this method of inquiry.[11] The idea of directly interviewing coachees (**Group 5**) and counselling clients (**Group 6**) also was considered but rejected for a number of reasons. First, gaining access to these populations is difficult. I would have had to get permission from the counsellors involved and they, in turn, would have to convince former clients to take part. To explore this idea, I held initial conversations with three counsellors. Each expressed a reluctance to participate. The concern was that clients would not want to speak about why they went for counselling and what they took from this because of privacy considerations: *"Research methodology is always a compromise between options ... choices are also frequently influenced by practical issues such as the availability of resources and the ability to get access to organisations and their memberships in order to undertake research"* (Gill & Johnson, 2010: 6). **Group 3** (executive coaching practitioners) and **Group 4** (counsellors and psychotherapists) were particularly important, so proportionately more people in both of these categories were interviewed. Two respondents were UK-based, adding some international counterweight to the mainly Irish experience reported.

Coachee Group: It would have been possible to access my own (former) coaching clients. The concern in working with this group was around reporting bias. Would coachees be fully open about their experiences? Would they inflate the importance of the work we'd done to make me feel good about the outcome? A second consideration under this heading (for both groups) was that the specialised nature of the topic offered no particular upside for either coachees or clients in getting access to the research findings - a normal part of the *quid pro quo* for taking part in a research project. While the findings are important for people working in this field, this audience is specialised. However, as coaching and counselling are private processes that cannot generally be observed, this poses the difficulty that information is *reported*. We therefore have to be careful about making definitive findings. It's also difficult to measure some outcomes – for example, an increase in self-awareness or happiness? Fortunately, there is an abundance of literature on these and related topics so I was able to access

---

[11]   Term coined in 1950 by Henry Landsberger when analyzing earlier experiments at the Hawthorne Works, a Western Electric factory outside Chicago.

this information (albeit indirectly) through a comprehensive literature review.

Gaining Access to Respondents: This part of the research proved relatively easy. Of the initial target listing (24 people), all agreed to take part. Two dropped out during the process, giving a 92% response rate. Initial contact was made by telephone and interview dates arranged. This was a more *personal* approach than contact by email and, perhaps, helps to explain the high participation rate. The vast majority of the dates stayed firm and interviews were conducted on schedule. Interviews lasted between 60 to 90 minutes (in three cases the interviews ran to over two hours). After each interview, a standard note of thanks was sent by email. In all cases, 'seasoned' practitioners were targeted, rather than people more recently qualified (to support data validity).

Research Location: Interviews were carried out at the person's place of work. The option of meeting outside of normal working hours was offered but declined. Getting interrupted by normal business was a potential negative, but in practice this posed little difficulty. In a small number of cases we encountered short interruptions, but it was relatively easy to get back on track when the interview resumed. For some telephone interviews I used Skype, which allowed a better connection (being able to see the respondents and *vice versa*).

Maintaining Confidentiality: An assurance was given to all respondents that confidentiality would be maintained. Once the initial slight hesitation was overcome and trust was built, the respondents were remarkably open in expressing their views and providing information / documentation about this topic. To maintain confidentiality, respondents are identified throughout this dissertation using an alphabetical code rather than being named.

Case Studies: To illustrate particular points, I've used a case approach. While client details have been changed to protect confidentiality, the accounts are factual in all other respects. The cases represent a *short-story* version of what happened – rather than a comprehensive review of each relationship. When dialog from coaching sessions is used, the notes were made either during the actual sessions or immediately afterwards. I've tried to capture faithfully what was actually said (as distinct from what I *should have said*). Well-reported case studies of successful and not-so-successful assignments perhaps don't meet the criteria of pure 'research'. Yet, some of the most important learning about coaching can be lost in research that solely focuses on correlation coefficients and statistical averages. Case studies help to prise open the 'closed door' that acts as a barrier to understanding coaching (Hall *et al*, 1999).

Literature Review: Given the variety of approaches to therapy (different schools) and the different *strands* of expertise within coaching, making sense of these broad topics was a key hurdle to be overcome. To support this, an extensive literature review was conducted in the libraries at University College Dublin (Michael Smurfit Business School), the National College of Ireland and the Irish Management Institute. In addition, the Chartered Institute of Personnel & Development library service in London provided a range of useful source materials.

Questionnaires: The questionnaires used were:

Group 1: Purchasers of Executive Coaching

- o Why does your organisation use executive coaching?
- o What criteria are important in the choice of provider? For example, professional training, membership of a professional body (accredited), knowledge of the industry, track record of the individual.
- o How do you check the above? How 'formal' is the checking process?
- o What is your understanding of the principal differences between coaching and counselling?
- o How do you 'select' internal candidates who would benefit from a *coaching* intervention? Is this primarily developmental or problem-solving oriented?
- o How would you select someone who would benefit from a *counselling* intervention?
- o Do clients select their own coach?
- o During each engagement are clear coaching objectives set?
- o Are the coaching engagements formally structured? For example, a set number of sessions?
- o Does the organisation 'see' the outputs from the coaching sessions? How is confidentiality managed?
- o Is the line / HR manager directly involved at any point?
- o What ROI is expected from coaching interventions? Any specific evaluation techniques?
- o Typically, how long does a coaching assignment last?
- o Typically, how much does a coaching assignment cost?
- o How often are clients declined by a coach (or referred to someone else) because the presenting issues lie outside of the training / skills / expertise of the coach?
- o What, if any, are your fears / concerns in deploying coaching? Have you seen poor outcomes or even 'damage' to a client? Examples ...
- o Will you continue to use coaching as part of your ongoing 'toolkit' of activities? ('more' or 'less'?)

Group 2: Purchasers of Counselling Services

o Does the organisation use external counsellors / therapists? Why?

o What criteria are important in the choice of provider? For example, professional training, membership of a professional body (accredited), knowledge of the industry, track record of the individual, choosing counsellors from particular psychology 'schools' or disciplines.

o What is your understanding of the principal differences between coaching and counselling?

o How are individual clients identified and selected for counselling?

o How would you differentiate this from someone who would benefit from a *coaching* intervention?

o Are clients allowed to select their own counsellor?

o Is each engagement based on clear objectives?

o Are the counselling engagements formally structured? For example, a set number of sessions?

o Does the organisation 'see' the outputs from the counselling sessions? How is confidentiality managed?

o What, if any, evaluation techniques are employed?

o Typically, how long does a counselling assignment last?

o Typically, how much does a counselling assignment cost?

o What are your fears / concerns in deploying counselling? Have you seen poor outcomes or even 'damage' to a client? Are there any obvious warning signs to look out for? Examples ...

o Will you continue to use counselling as part of your ongoing 'toolkit' of activities? ('more' or 'less')

Group 3: Executive Coaching Practitioners

o How did you become an executive coach?

o What specific training / qualifications do you have for this role?

o Are you a member of a professional coaching body?

o Do you operate a particular 'model'? For example, how people change, GROW, etc.).

o Do you follow a very structured process? How would you describe this?

o Do you use psychometric instruments? If so, what specific instruments do you use?

o Do you prepare formal 'coaching plans'? Who gets to see this?

o Typically, what are the 'presenting' issues you deal with?

o When you are working optimally, at your very best, what are you doing?

o Are the sessions limited to a set number of meetings or more open ended? What's typical?

o Does the organisation 'see' the outputs from these sessions? How is confidentiality managed? Does this pose any ethical conflicts for you?

o Do clients find the process useful / in what way? What, if any, evaluation techniques are employed?

o What is your understanding of the difference between the service you provide and that offered by therapists or counsellors?

o Are there areas you would consider to be 'off-limits' in terms of your practice? What?

o Have you ever refused to work with a client because of their 'presenting issues' or referred a client onto someone else because of presenting issues that emerged mid-contract?

o How much do you charge for your services? Who pays?

o Do you use any form of supervision for your executive coaching practice?

o What are your fears / concerns in working in this area? For example, poor outcomes, unable to unravel deep-seated issues, self-harm by the client.

Group 4: Counsellors and Psychotherapists

o How did you become a counsellor / therapist?

o What specific training / qualifications do you have for this role? How would you describe your specialism? For example, Psychodynamic; Person-Centered; Gestalt; PAC; Existentialism; CBT)

o Are you a member of a professional counselling body?

o Do you operate a particular 'model' based on a set of beliefs about how people change or what makes people function well mentally? For example, Appreciative Inquiry.

o Do you follow a very structured process? How would you describe this? For example, timeline, anxiety approaches, what happens 'in the room' etc.

o Typically, what are the 'presenting' issues you deal with?

o Are the sessions limited to a set number of meetings or more open ended? What's typical?

o Do clients find the process useful / in what way? What, if any, evaluation techniques are employed?

o When you are working optimally, at your very best, what are you doing?

o Are there some elements of the process that you intend to change going forward?

o   How much do you charge for your services? Who pays?

o   Where an organisation pays the fees, do they get to 'see' the outputs from the sessions? How is confidentiality managed?

o   Are there areas you would consider to be 'off-limits' in terms of your practice? What?

o   Have you ever refused to work with a client because of their 'presenting issues' or referred a client onto someone else because of presenting issues that emerged mid-contract?

o   What supervision do you use for your practice?

o   What are your fears / concerns in working in this area? For example, suicide, fear of litigation.

APPENDIX B: EXAMPLE AGREEMENT FOR COACHING SERVICES

Client Name: **Date:**

Address:

Phone:

Email:

Company:

Company Address:

Duration of Agreement:

Frequency of Coaching Sessions

As Needed: ___ Weekly: ___ Bi Monthly: ___ Quarterly: ___

Coaching Goals (examples listed)
> Personal leadership capacity
> Develop deeper self-belief and confidence
> Prepare for a future leadership role
> Build more effective teams
> Specific Skills (for example, time management or delegation skills)

Coaching Services
> One-to-one Coaching
> Recommend reading material and practices to support development

Fees: € hourly / daily rate:

Estimated: Time and engagement (specify).
Resources provided by the coach (specify).

Confidentiality:
> Completely confidential   _____
> Outcomes discussed with client organisation   _____

Compliance

By signing this service agreement, the client and the coach-consultant commit to following through with all the major components specified. In addition, any homework assignments or reasonable requests that are mutually agreed will be honoured to the best of the parties' abilities. Both the client and the coach agree to communicate clearly and address openly any problems, disagreements, or questions that arise during the duration of this coaching project.

CONSULTANT   DATE

CLIENT   DATE

ABOUT THE AUTHOR

Paul Mooney holds a Ph.D. and a Post-Graduate Diploma in Industrial Sociology (Trinity College). He also holds an M.Sc. and a Post-Graduate Diploma in Advanced Executive & Business Coaching (University College Dublin), along with a National Diploma in Industrial Relations (National College of Ireland). Paul is a Fellow of the Chartered Institute of Personnel & Development and is widely recognised as an expert on organisation and individual change.

Paul began his working life as a butcher in Dublin. After completing a formal apprenticeship, he moved into production management. He subsequently joined General Electric and held a number of human resource positions in manufacturing. After GE, Paul worked with Sterling Drug in Ireland and the Pacific Rim, with responsibility for all HR activity across Asia.

On return to Ireland, he established a management consulting company specialising in Organisation and Management Development. Between 2007 and 2010, Paul held the position of President,

National College of Ireland. He subsequently set up Tandem Consulting, a team of senior OD / Change specialists. Tandem's client list reads like a 'Who's Who' of Irish and multinational organisations with consulting assignments across 20+ countries – for both public and private sector clients.

Paul is the author of 11 books covering a wide span of issues and topics around organisation performance and personal change. Areas of expertise include:

o   Organisational Development / Change and Conflict Resolution.

o   Leadership Development / Executive Coaching.

o   Human Resource Management / Employee Engagement.

He writes a bi-weekly blog *'Confessions of a Consultant'*, which can be sourced at **http://tandemconsulting.wordpress.com**.

BOOKS BY PAUL MOONEY

Amie: The True Story of Adoption in Asia
Developing High Performance Organisations
The Effective Consultant
Keeping Your Best Staff
Turbocharging the HR Function
The Badger Ruse (crime novel)
Union Free: Creating a Committed and Competent Workforce
Desperate Executives: Coaching, Change and Personal Growth
Accidental Leadership: A Personal Journey
The Transformation Roadmap: Accelerating Organisation Change
Fog Clearance: Mapping the Boundary between Coaching and Counselling

OAK TREE PRESS

Oak Tree Press develops and delivers information, advice and resources for entrepreneurs and managers. It is Ireland's leading business book publisher, with an unrivalled reputation for quality titles across business, management, HR, law, marketing and enterprise topics. NuBooks is its ebook-only imprint, publishing short, focused ebooks for busy entrepreneurs and managers.

In addition, Oak Tree Press occupies a unique position in start-up and small business support in Ireland through its standard-setting titles, as well training courses, mentoring and advisory services.

Oak Tree Press is comfortable across a range of communication media – print, web and training, focusing always on the effective communication of business information.

OAK TREE PRESS
T: + 353 86 244 1633 / + 353 86 330 7694
E: info@oaktreepress.com
W: www.oaktreepress.com / www.SuccessStore.com.